T0327185

Make:
AI Robots

CREATE AMAZING ROBOTS WITH ARTIFICIAL INTELLIGENCE USING MICRO:BIT

By Reade Richard, Brenda Shivanandan,
Andy Forest, and Denzel Edwards

Foreword by Lorrie Ann Smith

Make:
AI ROBOTS

By Reade Richard, Brenda Shivanandan, Andy Forest, and Denzel Edwards

ISBN: 978-1-68045-729-2

November 2023: First Edition

See www.oreilly.com/catalog/errata.csp?isbn=9781680457292 for release details.

MAKE: BOOKS
President Dale Dougherty
Creative Director Juliann Brown
Editor Kevin Toyama
Designer Terisa Davis
Copyeditor Mark Nichol

Make: Community is a growing, global association of makers who are shaping the future of education and democratizing innovation. Through *Make:* magazine, 200+ annual Maker Faires, Make: books, and more, we share the know-how of makers and promote the practice of making in schools, libraries, and homes. Make: books may be purchased for educational, business, or sales promotional use. Online editions are also available for most titles. For more information, contact our corporate/institutional sales department at 800-998-9938.

Make Community, LLC
150 Todd Road, Suite 100
Santa Rosa, California 95407
www.make.co

A GUIDE FOR EDUCATORS AND PARENTS

By Lorrie Ann Smith
Vice President of Learning &
Engagement, Ontario Science Centre

We know that technology-based learning can open up a world of possibilities for children. In an era in which technology is transforming many aspects of our lives, we as educators and parents have the opportunity to embark on a journey of understanding alongside our children. Learning with tech tools like robotics and artificial intelligence (AI) can foster curiosity, creativity, and problem-solving skills. This means we can begin to prepare kids for a future where these skills are increasingly in demand, but more importantly, it means we can inspire a sense of fun, wonder, and empowerment, equipping the learner with the capability to shape the future through their own innovation and invention. It's not just about building machines; it's about young minds becoming architects of a technologically advanced and inclusive world.

Teachers, you are preparing these young architects of the future, shaping them for the challenges and opportunities ahead. Parents, you are the first and most influential teachers your children will ever have. Together, we can create safe spaces for risk-taking, failure, play, and inquiry. In doing so, we create the conditions for kids to have agency, to feel successful and supported, and to emerge curious and capable.

I was introduced to Andy and the team at Steamlabs in 2017 when we met to discuss a possible partnership with the organization I work for, the Ontario Science Centre. We were looking for a new kind of collaboration to help us achieve an experimental and ambitious project called the Inventorium — an informal learning experience designed to inspire co-creation through hands-on Maker activities and technology-based challenges that blur the boundaries between science and art. Little did I know that this would be the beginning of a yearslong collaboration between Steamlabs and the Ontario Science Centre that has included exhibit experiences and programs for thousands of kids, parents, and educators.

Through these projects and our incredible partnership with Steamlabs, we have been able to experiment and learn together, supporting and facilitating access to play- and inquiry-based learning environments. We have also been able to create safe spaces that encourage multiple points of entry, provide room to fail, and encourage active and creative collaboration.

Steamlabs is a dedicated nonprofit organization committed to empowering the next generation of learners by nurturing their curiosity, creativity, and critical thinking in the realms of science and technology. Their mission is to cultivate an inclusive and supportive learning environment that fosters agency, empathy, and collaboration among children from diverse backgrounds. By developing essential science, technology, engineering, art, and math (STEAM) and AI skills, Steamlabs aims to equip young minds with the confidence and knowledge to create, innovate, and actively participate in shaping a more equitable, ethical, and responsible society for all.

From the first Steamlabs summer camps in 2010, where the goal was to empower kids to create amazing things with technology, hundreds of thousands of children have built incredible projects in Steamlabs programs at science centers, libraries, schools, and makerspaces worldwide. Over the years, the Steamlabs mission has extended beyond merely making things into cultivating Makers. Steamlabs works to help children develop into capable, thoughtful citizens for the 21st century, empowering them to understand AI for their own use and advocate for equitable, ethical policies from companies and governments.

And in this book, Reade, Brenda, Andy, and Denzel have gathered some of the best projects to share — projects tested and inspired by the many other Steamlabs staff and participants over the years.

As you work together on the activities in this book, consider these tips from the team at Steamlabs to facilitate and enhance the learner experience.

Embrace a Playful, Inquiry-Based Approach

Encourage children to explore AI and robotics projects with curiosity, enthusiasm, and a playful attitude. Build an inquiry-based learning space, motivate kids to ask questions, seek answers, and investigate the world of AI and robotics. Create a safe and supportive environment for children to take risks, make mistakes, and learn from them.

Think of the projects as a starting point for the learners' imagination. You can get to something awesome quickly. Then it's up to you to take it from there! For example, in a facial-expression or sound-recognition project, encourage children to explore ways the robot can react to various expressions in a playful manner. Let them brainstorm and test out creative ideas for using this feature, such as creating a robot that displays jokes and responds to the sound of people's laughter or one that displays comforting words when it visually detects a sad face.

Focus on the Process and Encourage Reflection

Emphasize the learning process, skill development, creativity, and critical thinking over the end product of each project. Teach children the importance of iterating, reflecting, and learning from their experiences because in doing so, you are fostering a growth mindset.

For example, in the project for judging a marble race, provide guidance but allow children to make their own decisions about the robot's design and functionality. Encourage them to iterate on their design and reflect on what they learned from each iteration, such as improving the AI's accuracy in detecting the marbles or the stability and positioning of the camera during the race.

Support Learning and Embrace Diversity

Offer guidance and support when needed while allowing children to make their own discoveries and find solutions. Adjust your support as needed, recognizing that each child's learning journey is unique. Encourage diverse ideas and solutions, celebrating the different strengths, interests, and perspectives children bring to the projects.

Work alongside children to guide and support their creative journey without dictating the process. For example, in the coin-counting project, encourage them to share their unique ideas, such as creating a robot that collects coins for a treasure hunt or one that rewards trivia answers with coins. By celebrating the diversity of ideas and solutions, children will learn from one another and develop a deeper understanding of AI and robotics. In our testing of these projects, kids often came up with innovative ideas that we didn't yet know how to support. We spent time between sessions researching and preparing so we could guide them to refine their ideas and learn from similar projects.

Empower Learner Agency and Real-World Connections

Provide guidance while allowing children the autonomy to make their own discoveries and solve challenges independently. Help children recognize the relevance of AI and robotics in real-world contexts, inspiring them to use their newfound skills to create a positive impact on their communities and beyond.

In vision- and sound-recognition projects, provide guidance but allow children to make their own decisions about what the AI should "see" and "hear," as well as the physical robot's design and functionality. Encourage them to think about real-world scenarios in which object recognition could be useful, such as sorting recyclables for waste management or identifying plant species for environmental research. By connecting their projects to real-world situations, children will better understand the importance of their AI and robotics skills and feel empowered to create solutions that can make a positive impact.

Advocate for Responsible AI Practices and Ethics

Engage children in conversations about ethical considerations and responsible AI usage during their projects. Guide children in making well-informed decisions about AI design and application, nurturing empathy and social responsibility as they delve into the world of AI and robotics.

For example, in the project about facial-expression recognition, engage children in discussions about the ethical implications of AI-powered facial-expression recognition. Does how you look on the outside always match how you feel on the inside? What other implications does it have if AI treats people based solely on how they look? There are also privacy concerns and potential biases in AI-training data. Guide them in making responsible decisions about how their robot collects, processes, and stores data, as well as how it can be used fairly and without bias. By exploring the ethical dimensions of AI and robotics, children will develop a deeper understanding of their social responsibility as creators and users of technology.

The projects in this book are designed to be creative and fun. They also allow learners to strengthen productive work habits and increase self-confidence in science and technology. The activities outlined here can act as a gateway to deeper exploration of creativity and innovation and can foster logical and abstract reasoning skills, the ability to focus and process information, and development of productive learning habits. Think of AI as an assisting tool to help kids imagine, create, and engineer. Together with other tools and materials, it supports a playful and informal learning environment for children where they can have agency in their own learning with support from you. From there, the possibilities are endless!

As you support your children or students in their AI and robotics learning journey, remember that you play a key role in shaping their future and fostering a lifelong passion for creativity and innovation.

Let's embark on an exciting adventure together and get ready to witness some incredible AI bot creating!

To endless sparks of creativity,

Lorrie Ann Smith is the VP of learning and engagement at the Ontario Science Centre, one of the first interactive science museums in the world. She oversees the creation and implementation of all onsite experiences. Lorrie Ann previously served as the manager of young audience engagement and learning at the Art Gallery of Ontario, and taught courses at Ontario College of Design University, Boston University, and the University of Toronto.

CONTENTS

CONTENTS

6

GUMBALL MACHINE

7

SUPERHERO COSTUMES

8

ROBOT FRIENDS

Adobe Stock-drawlab19

An Introduction to the World of
AI Robots

Are you curious about how the world around you works? Do you enjoy tinkering with gadgets and electronics? If so, then you're in the right place! This book is all about exploring the exciting world of simple electronics and micro:bit projects — but it takes a step beyond by introducing artificial intelligence (AI) as a way to help your projects move on their own.

Even if you've never worked with electronics before, this book will guide you through the basics of circuitry and programming so you can create your own innovative and fun projects. Whether you want to build a robot that can navigate your room, a game that responds to your movements, or a gadget that can recognize your voice, this book has everything you need to get started. So get ready to unleash your creativity and dive into the exciting world of AI-enhanced electronics!

THE GAME PLAN

We've got some amazing projects lined up for you, and they all have one thing in common: They're designed to help you learn through hands-on experiences. By building your very own AI robots, you'll explore the exciting world of electronics, coding, and AI, all while having a blast and developing valuable skills.

Each project in this book is divided into four parts:

1. **Basic Build:** Create an awesome foundation for your project using cardboard and other recyclable materials.
2. **Electronics:** Add cool electronic components like LEDs, motors, and buzzers to enhance your projects.
3. **Micro:bit:** Use simple coding and a micro:bit to control your electronics and make your project come to life.
4. **AI:** Train an AI to give your project some extra smarts and capabilities, enabling it to react to the world around it.

Each section builds on the previous one, slowly but steadily teaching and providing practice of new skills. The projects are designed so you can work at your own speed and come back to more advanced stages when you're ready to challenge yourself. You can also mix and match the different stages and customize them according to your interests and abilities.

So don't be afraid to customize, experiment, and let your imagination run wild; it's all about the process and the skills you develop, not just the final result!

GATHER YOUR MATERIALS AND TOOLS

Before you start building your awesome AI robots, make sure you have all the materials and tools you'll need. We're going to use as many recyclable materials as possible, so keep an eye out for things you can find around your house. Here are some ideas:

- Corrugated cardboard from packages
- Thin cardboard, like cereal boxes or milk cartons
- Paper towel rolls
- Straws
- Wooden sticks, like craft dowels or chopsticks

Using recyclable materials is not only eco-friendly but also means you can easily reuse them for other projects in the future.

Now let's gather some extra supplies that will help us put everything together:

- Rubber bands
- Paper clips and other fasteners
- Popsicle sticks
- Construction paper
- Pencils
- Blank paper

It's important to have the right tools for building your projects. Here's a list of some basic tools you'll need:

- Scissors
- Glue
- Tape
- Hole punch

And with an adult's help, you can also use the following:

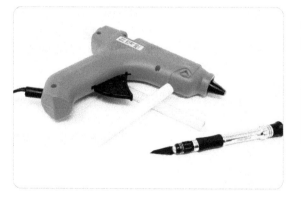

- Glue gun
- X-Acto knife

For your workspace, find a flat and clutter-free area like a desk, dinner table, or even the floor. Make sure that you have enough room to move around, your materials and tools are within reach, and there's an adult nearby to help if needed. Even if you're a messy person, try to keep your workspace organized and neat to avoid the frustration of misplaced materials and parts.

STENCIL LIBRARY

To help guide these projects, we've created some **stencils**, or patterns, for a project's craft components. They're available as free downloadable PDFs at:

- makeairobots.com/chapter1
- makeairobots.com/chapter2
- makeairobots.com/chapter3
- makeairobots.com/chapter4
- makeairobots.com/chapter5
- makeairobots.com/chapter6
- makeairobots.com/chapter7
- makeairobots.com/chapter8

These stencils can be printed and glued onto cardboard and then cut out to make building your projects easier.

Notes:

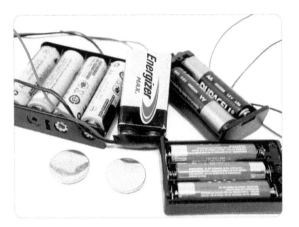

BASIC ELECTRONIC COMPONENTS

Before we jump into building our cool AI robots, let's explore some of the electronics you'll be using along the way:

Batteries and Circuits

Batteries are like the heart of your project — they give it the energy it needs to work! When you connect the two ends of a battery with a wire or a device that needs power, electricity flows from the positive terminal through the device and back to a battery's negative terminal in a path called a **circuit**. If a circuit isn't complete, your device won't get the power it needs to work.

Wires and Copper Tape

Copper is an excellent conductor of electricity, which is why it's used to make wires. In this book, we'll be using thin jumper wires to create connections between our electronic components. Sometimes these will have different ends: There can be a pin, a socket, or even a set of metal teeth. (This type is known as **alligator wire**, with an **alligator clip**.) These are different ways these wires can connect to projects, and they're all incredibly easy to use.

Copper tape is another way to conduct electricity. It's just a flat, sticky version of copper wires that we can use to create superthin pathways for our circuits.

LEDs

Light-emitting diodes (LEDs) use energy to create little particles of light called photons. Depending on the materials used in making the LED, we can see these photons in a variety of colors.

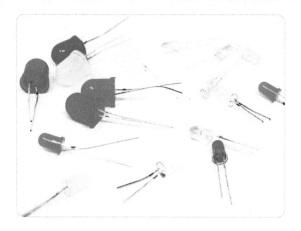

When working with LEDs, it's important to remember that they allow energy to flow only in one direction: from the longer, positive leg to the shorter, negative leg. If an LED isn't working, check whether you've mistakenly connected the positive wire to the positive leg and the negative wire to the negative leg — it's easy to mix them up.

Buzzers and Speakers

These devices can turn electrical energy into sound waves, enabling our projects to make noise and even play sounds and music! Buzzers create simple beeps, while speakers can produce more complex sounds.

Servo Motor

Servo motors contain a tiny chip — called a driver — that enables us to control them using signals from a computer or a micro:bit. These small motors are great for precise movements and light tasks, but they might not be strong enough to move heavy objects.

DC Motors and Geared Motors

DC (direct current) motors use magnets to spin a central shaft, which can be used to move other components like wheels at high speeds.

Geared motors use gears to increase their strength at the cost of speed, making them useful for heavier tasks that move

more slowly. These gears are usually inside a plastic casing to protect them.

Now that we have a basic understanding of the electronics we'll be using, we're one step closer to building our awesome AI robots!

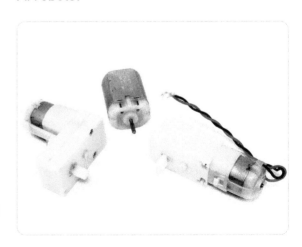

Notes:

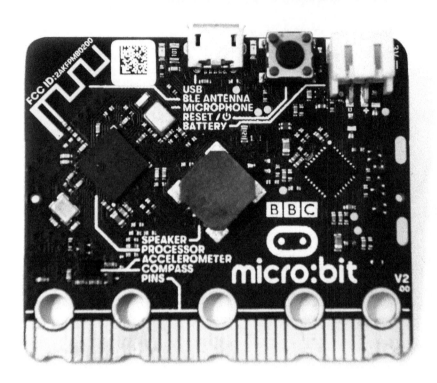

USB
BLE ANTENNA
MICROPHONE
RESET / ⏻
BATTERY

SPEAKER
PROCESSOR
ACCELEROMETER
COMPASS
PINS

BBC
micro:bit
V2

DIVE INTO MICRO:BIT AND CODING

In our projects, we'll be using a tiny but powerful computer called a **micro:bit**. This little device is perfect for experimenting with coding, and it's super easy to use!

The micro:bit is a **microcontroller**, a miniature computer that can be programmed to control other electronic components like LEDs, motors, and sensors. It's perfect for inventing cool gadgets and learning about coding at the same time!

GETTING TO KNOW YOUR MICRO:BIT

When you look closely at your micro:bit, you may notice a few important things:

• The square of little dots on the front is actually a grid of 25 tiny LED lights. You can easily tell the micro:bit to turn each

LED on and off, giving you the ability to display numbers, letters, or even pictures with these lights.

- The two little buttons on either side are some simple inputs that will give us an easy way to tell our micro:bit to follow a command, like playing a tune or resetting a counter.
- The five metal holes at the bottom, called **pins**, are used to connect to electronic devices.
  - **Pin 0, 1, and 2:** These are the individual "arms" of the micro:bit, where you can use different lines of code to control whatever we connect here.

- **3V and GND:** These are used for power. When connecting a device, the positive wire connects to the 3 V (3-volt) pin, while the negative wire connects to the GND (ground) pin to create a controllable circuit.

This little piece of hardware is going to become the brain in your projects. You'll use it for all sorts of tasks, from controlling your motors to helping you keep track of times and scores.

To program the micro:bit, we'll be using a free website called MakeCode, which

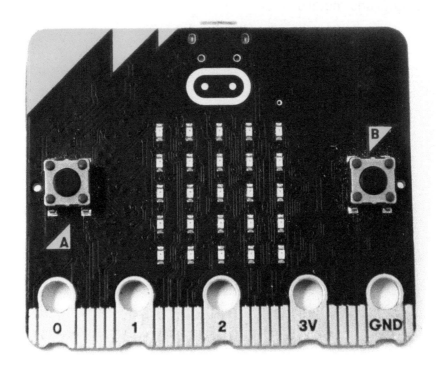

you can access from any web browser. This website uses the coding language Blockly, which enables you to create code by combining colorful building blocks together like puzzle pieces. This makes it really easy to learn, even if you've never tried coding before.

The MakeCode website is located at makecode.microbit.org.

Throughout this book, we'll show you how to use the MakeCode website to program your micro:bit and bring your AI robot projects to life. You'll learn how to create code that responds to different inputs, like button presses or voice commands, and controls various outputs, like lights and motors.

Each chapter shows how to build the code for a particular project, and includes a Code Library to help visually identify the code blocks so you'll know exactly which piece to use.

Learning to code is an amazing skill to have, and it can open up a world of creative possibilities. By the end of this book, you'll have the knowledge and confidence to create all sorts of cool projects using the micro:bit and Blockly.

Notes:

 **AI**

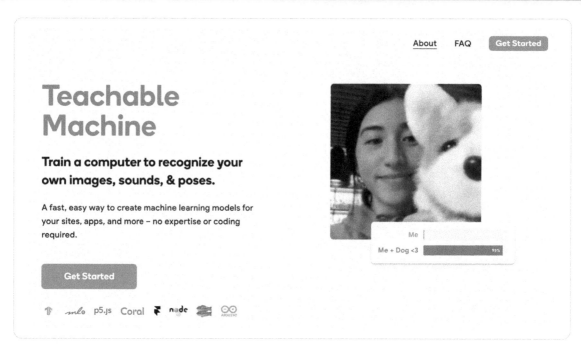

EXPLORING THE WORLD OF AI

Get ready to dive into the fascinating world of AI! After you've crafted your projects, hooked them up to electronics, and programmed the micro:bit to control our creations, you'll learn how to use AI to make these projects smarter and more interactive. By understanding AI and how we can use it in your projects, you'll unlock a new tool with endless opportunities to explore.

So, what exactly is **AI**? "**Artificial intelligence**" refers to a computer's ability to perform tasks usually associated with human intelligence, like recognizing images and patterns and understanding sounds and spoken words. AI systems can analyze data, make observations, and draw conclusions to interact with the world around them, just like we do!

AI is already a big part of our daily lives. It helps recommend music on streaming platforms, gives us turn-by-turn directions on phone apps, and even supports important fields like healthcare and environmental conservation. As AI continues to evolve and become more common, it's important for people to understand how it works and its potential benefits and limitations. This knowledge will help you use AI as a tool in your life and think critically about its ethical and societal implications.

Throughout this book's projects, you'll integrate AI with cardboard creations to bring them to life. You will do this by using AI tools like Google's Teachable Machine and your micro:bit controllers to teach your robots to recognize objects, sounds, and even facial expressions to make your projects interactive and responsive to their environment.

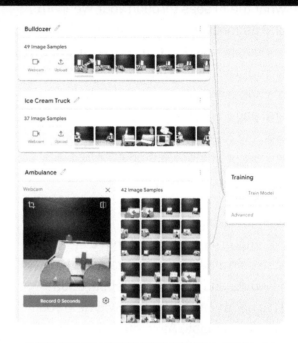

Teachable Machine is a web-based platform that lets you train AI models using your computer's webcam and microphone. With this tool, you can teach your AI to recognize different objects, sounds, or body poses, which can then be used to control your micro:bit-enabled robots.

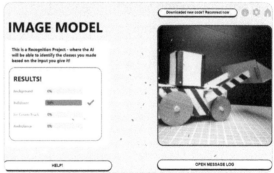

For example, if you want your project to recognize an ambulance, you'll use your webcam to take lots of pictures of an ambulance from different angles and distances. This data will teach the AI what an ambulance looks like and help your AI model become more accurate at distinguishing an ambulance from other vehicles, like a bulldozer or an ice cream truck.

Once you've trained your AI model, you will connect it to your micro:bit through a special Make AI Robots website at makeairobots.com.

This site acts as a translator between the AI and the micro:bit, showing you what the AI sees through your webcam and its most accurate prediction. More importantly, it also sends that information to your micro:bit. With some special lines of code (which you can find on page xxxiii, and page 107), you'll be able to use this website to activate the motors and lights in your projects, creating AI-infused machines.

By integrating AI into your projects, you'll not only bring your creations to life but also gain a deeper understanding of how AI works and its potential applications. This hands-on experience will help you develop valuable AI-related skills and better prepare you for a future in which AI plays an increasingly significant role in our lives and work.

KEY WEBSITES

Bookmark these three free websites because you will use them in each chapter!

- **MakeCode:**
  Program your micro:bit:
  makecode.microbit.org

- **Teachable Machine:**
  Create and train your AI:
  teachablemachine.withgoogle.com

- **Make AI Robots:**
  Download your trained AI to your micro:bit:
  makeairobots.com

READY? SET? MAKE!

Before we dive in, let's talk about something really important: It's totally OK to face challenges, and even fail. In fact, you *should* fail sometimes — that means you're trying something new. And trying new things is what makes this journey so exciting and fun!

Maybe your robot isn't moving the way you want it to, or your code just isn't working. Part of the inventing process is to test, redesign, and improve your projects. All the best inventions go through this prototyping stage, and it's an opportunity to reflect on your work and learn from your experiences. Don't be afraid of making mistakes — that's how you grow as a maker!

Kids: Always remember that an adult is there to help when needed, but you're the boss here — if you want to veer off a project's instructions, give it a shot. If it doesn't work, you can always come back to the original instructions!

Parents: This is a great opportunity to see the amazing things your child can do. It's great if they complete a project, but it's even better if they customize it with their own flourishes. Try to be as hands-off as possible, and let their creativity soar!

Here are a few helpful tips to keep in mind:
- **Take a step back:** If you're stuck, take a break and come back to the project later. You might discover a new solution with fresh eyes!
- **Ask for help:** Remember, you're not alone! Reach out to a parent, teacher, or friend if you need some guidance or a new perspective.
- **Learn from your mistakes:** Solving problems is a skill that improves with practice. Make a mistake? Figure out how to avoid repeating it. Embrace these opportunities to grow and become an even better inventor!
- **Keep experimenting:** Don't be afraid to try different approaches or change your design. We want you to not just complete our projects but also make them even better!

CONNECTING THE MICRO:BIT — DO NOT SKIP THIS PART!

It's important to remember that while the micro:bit and AI are both amazing pieces of technology, they are different technologies and need some help for them to work together. In order for your micro:bit and the AI to talk to each other, you're going to need a bit of *starter code*.

This starter code enables the micro:bit to understand the data being sent from the the Teachable Machine website, the place where you create and train your AI for a particular project.

In chapters 1–3, as you learn the basics of coding, use this preassembled starter code to enable your AI projects to work.

By chapter 4, you'll have learned the basics of coding and understand how the code blocks work, and we'll show you how to make the starter code yourself. But until then, you can simply use the preassembled code here to join in the fun!

Get your AI starter code here:
bit.ly/AIStarterCode

Notes:

1
HINGES, WINGS & FLYING THINGS

To start us off on our inventioneering journey, let's take a look at a basic simple machine that you use almost every day — the **hinge**. A hinge is something that connects two objects and helps them rotate. Just take a peek at the nearest door: That circular bar between the wall and the door is what enables it to rotate, or swing, open and close. Hinges are incredibly useful when building a robot, because they're a simple way to enable movement and transform a boring, static object into something more.

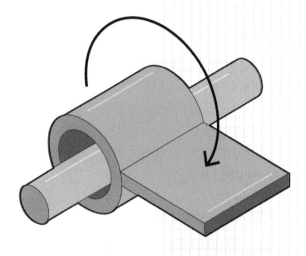

In this chapter, we're going to use hinges to create two of our favorite animals with flapping wings: butterflies and bats. We'll start with a simple and quick cardboard creation, using hinges and construction paper to make movable wings. After that, we'll use a battery, copper tape, and LEDs to create a simple circuit that adds glowing antennas or eyes!

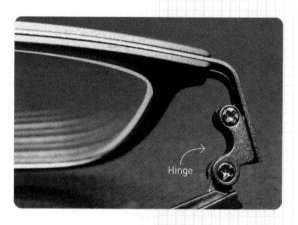

Hinge

CHALLENGE CHECKLIST:

- **Create a Bat or Butterfly with flapping wings**
- **Give our creation some glowing eyes or antennae**
- **Connect a micro:bit to give our creature a face**
- **Use AI to teach our critter to show emotions**

Hinge

Adobe Stock-DLefryandi and Elenapro

YOU WILL NEED:

- Stencils*
- Corrugated cardboard
- Glue
- Chopsticks, straws, or wooden dowels
- Hole punch
- Construction paper

For this and other projects, make sure you have all the materials close at hand in your workspace so you'll have everything you need to begin.

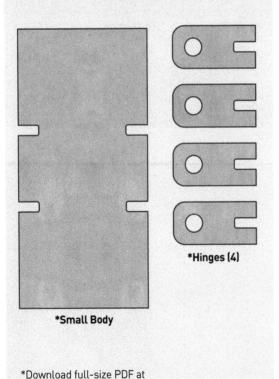

*Hinges (4)

*Small Body

*Download full-size PDF at Makeairobots.com/chapter1.

We'll then add a micro:bit to our creation, and learn how to blend art and technology on the micro:bit's big LED screen to add a face that can express emotions.

Finally, we'll add AI to our creation to really bring it to life. We'll train an audio-recognition AI to listen to and understand things you say, and this will enable your creation to react to your emotions: You can say, "Happy" or even just laugh out loud, and your creature will show its smiling face, or if you say, "Sad" or start crying, it will display a frowning face. Or make up your own faces and expressions, like surprise or even feeling fabulous — you're limited only by your imagination!

Looking around your workspace, you may already have a few ideas for materials to use to make some hinges. Tape is probably the most common and easiest to use, but if you've tried this method, you already know it's not very sturdy or reliable.

We can do much better than a flimsy connection like that. For this project, we can use the designs from our Stencil Library (see page xviii) to help us get started by building the body of the robot, and then create some hinges to enable it to move its wings!

1. The first step in this — and all future — projects is to trace the stencils onto paper, glue them onto cardboard, and cut them out. And whether you're using chopsticks, straws, or wooden dowels as connector rods, cut them to the length of the body; you'll use these later (Figure **1**).

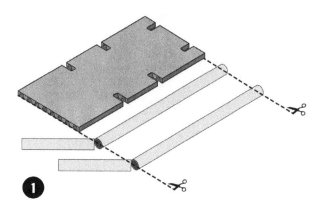

2. Take the four Straight Hinges that you made and slide them into the four slots on the side of the Small Body. Use a little bit of glue if it doesn't fit snugly (Figure **2**).

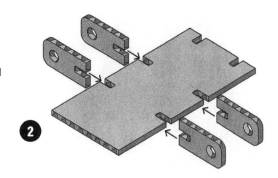

When they've all been tightly placed, it should look something like the image at the bottom right (Figure **3**).

3. Now take that connector rod you cut earlier and slide it through the holes in the hinges. To stop the connecting rods from sliding back through the holes, wrap some tape around the four ends of the rods; this creates a

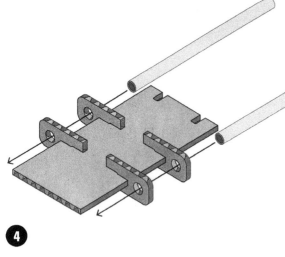

4

bulge that prevents the connecting rods from accidently slipping out of the hinge holes (Figures ❹ and ❺).

4. Finally, design wings for your creation. Whether you're making a bat, a butterfly, or your own creation, remember to design long strips on the end of your wings: These will wrap around the connector rods and be taped on the underside of the wing, holding it all together.

Cut out your wings and affix them to the connecting rods. If you don't have tape, you can use some glue — just make sure you give it enough time to dry! (Figures ❻ and ❼).

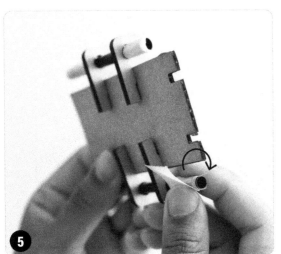

5

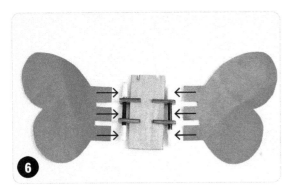

6

7

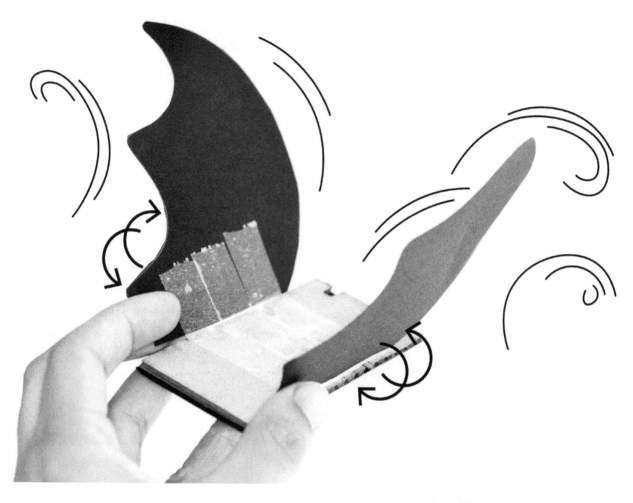

TAKING IT FURTHER

Now is your chance to jazz this up with some construction paper or other supplies you have lying around to give it your own personal touch! Of course, this is just one way to make a hinge for a project. Look around your workspace to see if you have any other materials that could make a good hinge.

ELECTRONICS

YOU WILL NEED:

- Basic Build body
- Thin cardboard, like a cereal box
- Copper tape
- Some LEDs (any size works; we use 5 mm here)
- 1.5 V coin cell battery, like a CR2032 or CR2025

Now that we have a basic creature body to work with, let's add a spark of electricity to bring it to life. As you can see, we've designed a fancier body after completing our Basic Build. It's based on the general

Small Body stencil, but with some curves to form a slightly more realistic head and body, and long antennae for fun.

Our project has a more straightforward shape for simplicity, but we're showing an example of how you can use the concepts we're teaching in your own creative ways.

1. The first step will be creating a button on the bottom of your creature out of thin cardboard, which will enable you to turn the lights on and off. You'll need a long strip of thin cardboard that can wrap from the top of the body over to the bottom.

   Start with the body flipped over so the bottom faces up. Glue half of the thin cardboard strip to the top of the body (the button mechanism will be hidden on the bottom of the body), but let it extend out to the back. You'll fold this over later to press down on the battery (Figure **8**).

2. Apply the copper tape over a large area on both sides of the head — just make sure the two sides do not touch. This is where we will mount the LEDs. If your copper tape is

narrow, you can use multiple strips; just make sure they slightly overlap each other. (Figure **9**).

3. Finish the bottom by cutting a small, circular pad of copper tape for the battery to sit on near the back (where the thin cardboard will fold over and press the battery). Connect that circle of copper tape to the LED-mounting area with a strip of copper tape (Figures **10** and **11**).

   If your tape strip breaks, don't worry — it's OK to use shorter strips and put them together as long as they overlap. Remember: building things is rarely neat and tidy, especially when you're experimenting!

4. It's time to mount your LEDs; you can use different colors, but remember that different-colored LEDs draw different amounts of power so your color choices will affect the brightness.

   Keep in mind that electricity flows in one direction (discussed in 'batteries and circuits page xx), so make sure the LED's short leg (—) is on the

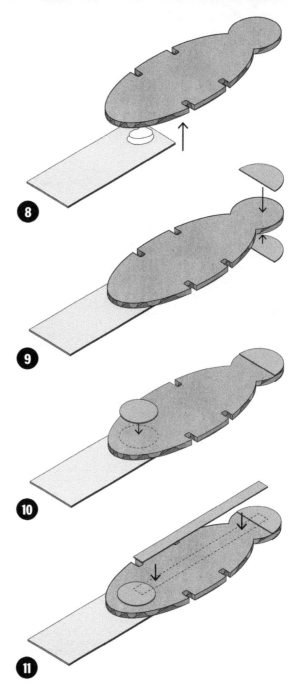

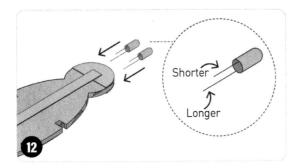

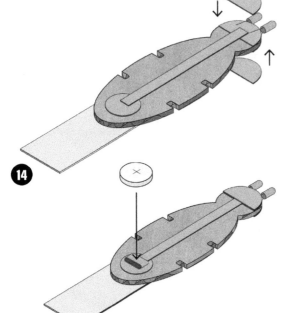

same side where the battery will sit and the longer leg (+) is on the nonbattery side (Figures ⑫ and ⑬).

When they're in place, cover the LED legs with more copper tape on each side to make sure the circuit is secure. It's OK to use more than one piece of copper tape and to have the tape extend over both legs on the same side — just make sure the top and bottom pieces of copper tape don't creep over the edge and touch the *other* side (Figure ⑭)!

5. Now it's time to add the battery. Make a tiny loop of copper tape and place it on the circular pad; we can use this to hold the battery in place. Make sure the negative side of the battery — the rough side — is the one you're taping down (Figures ⑮ and ⑯).

6. The final step is to complete the circuit on the other side with more copper tape. Flip your creation over so the battery is facing down. Apply a long

strip of copper tape that starts at the LED mounting area and continues down the length of the body, over the thin cardboard strip and over to the other side of the thin cardboard (Figure **17**).

You should now be able to fold the thin cardboard over the battery so the copper tape can touch the top and complete the circuit. If it's having issues staying connected, just add more copper tape where the tape will touch the battery top (Figures **18** and **19**).

When the cardboard is folded over and the copper tape touches the battery, there is now an uninterrupted flow of electrons through the circuit. Release the makeshift button and the circuit will be open, stopping power and turning off the lights. Congratulations, you made a simple circuit and added controllable lights to your creation!

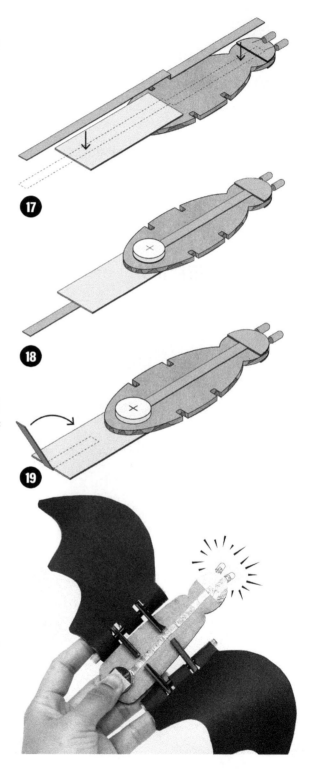

TAKING IT FURTHER

Take a moment to step back and admire the glowbug you just made. Copper tape is an amazing material to use when you want to create simple circuits on projects like these. We'll explore some more fun ways to use this in later chapters, so if you want a bit more practice, why not create a few more unique creatures to show off?

MICRO:BIT

YOU WILL NEED:
- Micro:bit
- USB cable
- Computer with internet access

Find starter and finished micro:bit code for guidance at: makeairobots.com/chapter1

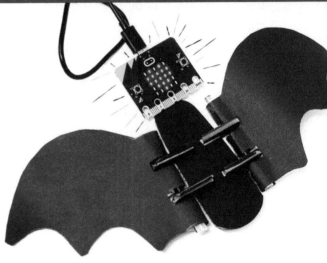

CODE LIBRARY

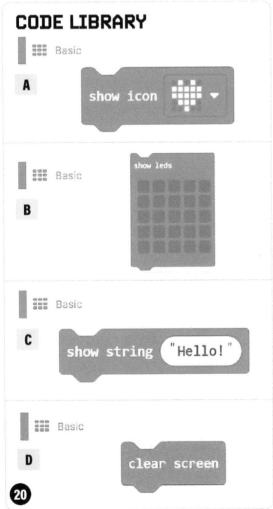

::: Basic

A

show icon

::: Basic

B

show leds

::: Basic

C

show string "Hello!"

::: Basic

D

clear screen

20

Hey, look at that! You've reached the first coding lesson. In this project, we're going to show you a simple way to add some real personality to your creation by giving it a face! We'll use code to design a face on a computer, attach our micro:bit to our robot, then upload the face to the micro:bit. Actually, *you're* going to do this — and we're going to show you how!

But first, we want to introduce you to the reference Code Library (boxes **A**, **B**, **C**, and **D** in Figure **20**). You'll see one of these at the start of every micro:bit section. This is a handy way of showing each code block used in a specific project, as well as where to find it on the MakeCode website, where we will build our code.

Think of the code blocks as unique tools that do a specific task. They are neatly organized at makecode.microbit .org in virtual drawers of a toolbox. For instance, the Show Icon code block **A** is located in the Basic drawer, while other code blocks are in the Input, Music, and other drawers, which we'll explore in later chapters.

Remember, your micro:bit is really just a tiny computer, complete with a CPU brain, and even tiny LED lights on the front to display information. We're going to use those tiny lights to create our robot's face, but first we need to tell the micro:bit how to do it.

To begin coding, first you're going to need to visit makecode.microbit.org. (See page xxiv). Click on the big purple New Project button, and you'll be taken to a new page with two blocks waiting for code; now we're all set to get started (Figure ㉑)!

1. These two blocks on the screen will serve as the backbone for most of your projects going forward. Whatever code we place into the Forever block will run . . . well,

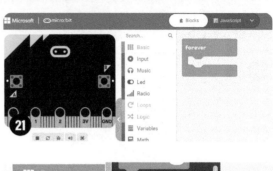

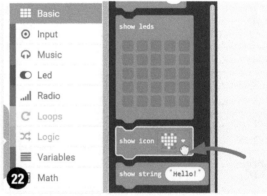

forever! This command will run your code on a loop over and over again once you start up.

(The On Start command will also run your code when the micro:bit starts up, but only once. Drag the On Start block over to the menu on the side to delete it — we won't need it for this lesson.)

2. Off to the left side, click on the Basic drawer at the top of the list to open it and reveal all the other code blocks there (Figure ㉒).

23

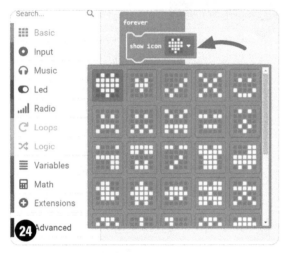

24

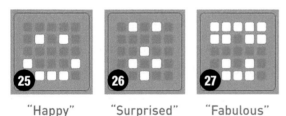

25 "Happy" **26** "Surprised" **27** "Fabulous"

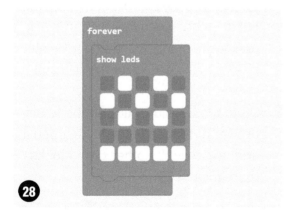

28

3. All we need to do is drag the third block, labeled Show Icon **A** , and place that into the mouth of the Forever block.

   If you accidentally misplace or delete a block, don't worry — you can always get another one in the block's drawer (Figure **23**).

4. You should see the little test screen on the left side pop to life after a second; this is a virtual version of your micro:bit screen to test your code.

   But . . . that's still not a face; it's the default heart. If you click on the little upside-down triangle next to the heart image in the code block, you'll find a whole bunch of face options available (Figures **24**, **25**, **26**, and **27**).

5. If you're feeling artistic, you can use the Show LEDs **B** block instead of the Show Icon **A** block, and design your own face by clicking on the individual dots of the Show LEDs **B** block (Figure **28**)!

DOWNLOADING

Are you ready to bring this code from the website into the palm of your hands? If you're happy with the way your project runs, give your project a name and save it to your computer using the disk icon next to the Download button at the bottom of the web page.

Now you're ready to get the code onto your micro:bit, and we can do this either of two ways.

Pairing

The first method is to pair your micro:bit with the website — this way, information can be sent back and forth easily. Using

the pairing method eliminates the need to remember to download your code to a specific folder in your micro:bit each time you change your code.

Connect your micro:bit to your computer using a USB cable. Click on the little gear icon in the top right of the window, and you'll find the option Connect Device (Figure **29**).

Direct Download

Some internet browsers don't allow Pairing, but that's OK — we can still use the Direct Download method.

Connect your micro:bit...

First, make sure your micro:bit is connected to your computer with a USB cable.

Next

Connect your micro:bit...

Pair your micro:bit to the computer by selecting 'BBC micro:bit CMSIS-DAP' or 'DAPLink CMSIS-DAP' from the popup that appears after you press the 'Next' button below.

29

Next

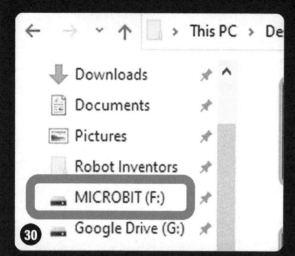

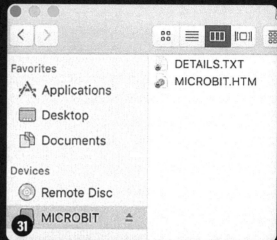

Click on the three-dots icon next to the Download button on the bottom left corner of the web page, and follow the Download as File instructions to save your code to your computer. When that has finished, open a window on your computer and search for a drive or location labeled Microbit.

On a Windows computer, it will look like the image at above left (Figure ③⓪).

On an Apple computer, it will look like the image at above right (Figure ③①).

When you've found this folder, simply drag and drop the file you downloaded from the Mak: AI Robots website (it will have a ".hex" suffix) into the Microbit folder on your computer. Moving your downloaded

file here will upload it from your computer to your micro:bit — it just adds a step compared to the Pairing method.

You will see the lights on the back blink really fast for a few seconds; when it stops, your code file has been uploaded to your micro:bit. You're all set!

All that is left is to attach the micro:bit to our creation. You can use whatever is available, such as tape, rubber bands, or even a binder clip or paper clip — just be careful not to damage your micro:bit!

And remember that we're going to use the micro:bit again, so avoid using glue or other mounting methods that may be problematic to remove.

TAKING IT FURTHER

In addition to faces, we can use a helpful little code block to show words on the screen as well. The Show String block in the Basic drawer gives us a way to type words or sentences that will slowly scroll across the screen. (A *String* is just coding slang for a sequence of characters or letters that the code uses as information.)

Try adding a Show String **C** block and adding your own text into the block's white field. You can also add a Clear Screen **D** block between the Show Icon **A** and Show String **C** blocks to switch back and forth between the face and words. This Clear Screen **D** block will make the screen go blank before moving onto the next screen and prevents screen changes from blending together.

YOU WILL NEED:

- Micro:bit
- USB cable
- Microphone
- Computer with internet access

For links to the AI tools, explore resources at:
makeairobots.com/chapter1

First we built a creature that has flapping wings. Then we used electronics to add fun lights and a micro:bit to add facial expressions. Are you ready for the final step? It's time to add some AI to our critter to really bring it to life!

We're going to train an AI model to recognize words like *happy* and *sad*, and show the appropriate expression on the micro:bit screen. Some special code will basically enable your robot to hear the words you're saying and determine what "face" it should wear.

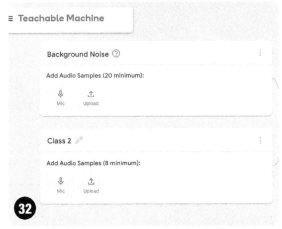

THE TRAINING

Our first task is to give this AI some data to learn. And all of this learning is going to happen on Google's Teachable Machine website (see page xxviii), located at teachablemachine.withgoogle.com.

We want to make your creature respond to your voice, so after clicking on the Get Started button on the website, click on the Audio Project button. This will open a new training module where you'll need to have your microphone front and center, ready to record (Figure ③).

1. The first thing this site asks from us is to record 20 seconds of background noise — this means you're going to have to be quiet and let the computer learn what "no one speaking" sounds like. This enables the Teachable Machine to learn what your room sounds like so it can focus directly on your words instead of the background noise of the room.

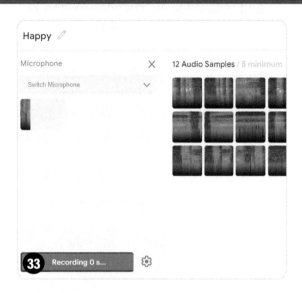

2. Click on the microphone button and then the Record 20 Seconds button, and sit back and wait. When you have 20 seconds of quiet time, you'll see an Extract Sample button. This will add your background-noise sample to the AI so it will have the first chunk of data it needs to learn.

▶ 00:00 / 00:20   Extract Sample

3. Just below that section, click the tile that reads Class 2 and name it after the emotion you want your creation to show; we're going to name this one Happy.

   This **class** (a group of similar data) requires much shorter samples than your 20 seconds of background noise, but you still need quite a few of them — remember, the more samples you add, the smarter your AI becomes.

So test out your acting skills by trying out different ways to say, "Happy": Say it in a funny voice, say it slower, say it like a question, etc., and click the Extract Sample button when each is completed. When you have about eight or nine of these variations recorded, you can move on to adding another class of sounds (Figure 33).

4. Click on the gray Add a Class button at the bottom of the web page to add more data sets for your AI, like Surprised or Fabulous. Add as many

classes as you like — just remember to give each class a different name, and repeat the instructions in step 2 to record them (Figure **34**).

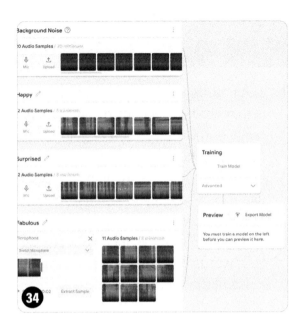

5. When you have all of your classes ready to learn, start the learning process by clicking the Train Model button in the middle column (Figure **35**). (If you don't have enough sounds in any of these classes, you will be reminded to add more.)

The Teachable Machine will take a few minutes to study and learn from the information you gave it. (See page xxviii). When the model is ready, you'll see the AI spring to life in the third column, labeled Preview. If you now say your word into the microphone, you will see a percentage reflecting how well the AI has learned your words.

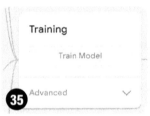

Test this out by saying your word — is it registering at 50%? 79% 100%? If it's not making the right selections, the AI may not have enough good information to recognize your words. Add more data into each class and train it again (Figure **36**).

6. When you're happy with the results of your smart AI, the last step is to save it: Click on the Export Model

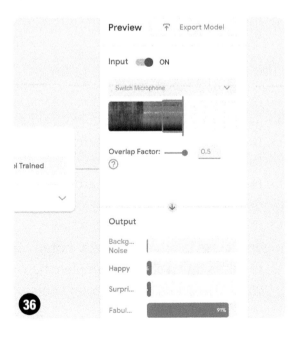

button in the Preview column, which will bring up a window, then select Upload Model. (This saves your AI model to the cloud, but your audio samples stay on your computer only). Copy the shareable URL link it provides so you can use it after you set up some micro:bit code to make sense of this data.

Open up a new browser window (so we can come back to this page if we need to retrain the AI), and go to makecode.micro:bit.org to get started (Figure **37**).

THE CODE

Now that your AI is smart enough to choose an emotion, we'll need to give it something to express that emotion: just two short steps, you will create different LED faces to show off all those classes, and then you'll create a way for the code to choose which face to use.

1. Open the saved AI Code file we made on page xxxiii (Figure **38**).

This is the code we described in the introduction that allows the programmed AI and micro:bit to speak to each other. From here, we should be able to add some familiar blocks to make faces.

Do you remember how to draw a face with the LEDs (see page 12)? You can either select one that's already made with Show Icon **A** or use the Show LEDs **B** tool and draw your own. Make a face for each class you made on the AI training site.

2. But where can we put these faces? Do you remember what part of this code tells your micro:bit what to do when the AI makes a prediction (Figure **39**)?

This If Statement block reads the data that we saved from the AI. If you change the " " text bubble to one of the class names you made (like Happy), then whenever the AI sends that signal to the micro:bit, it will activate whatever code we add underneath it. Place the smiling-face LED block in this spot, and you're almost done (Figures **40** and **41**)!

3. Now repeat this for each class you trained the AI to recognize. To give yourself more If statements to work with, click on the circled + icon in the bottom left corner of the block (Figure **42**). Copy (or duplicate this SerialData = block to use it again.

And that's all we need to do to code this project. If you created a lot of emotions for your AI, your code might get pretty long. That's OK — the micro:bit has enough memory to handle it. Just make sure that the names you type into Make: AI Robots website *exactly* match the class names you trained.

Now that this is all set up, let's jump over to https://makeAIRobots.com to see how everything works together.

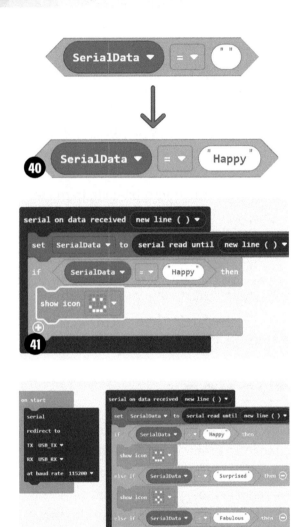

BRINGING IT TO LIFE

After connecting your micro:bit to your computer with a USB cable, we're on the doorstep of the Make: AI Robots website — the bridge that will help the AI speak with the micro:bit!

1. Click on the big Connect Your Micro:bit to Your AI button in the middle of the page. A small window will pop up, asking you to pair your micro:bit similar to how we did it on the Make: AI Robots website (Figure **43**).

There may be a few things in this list depending on what's plugged into your computer, but you're looking for the one that looks like this:

    mbed Serial Port (COM9) - Paired

"Mbed Serial Port [your COM number will be different]"

Once your micro:bit is successfully connected, you'll be taken to the next page (Figure **44**).

2. Remember that link we got from the Teachable Machine website? Copy and paste that here and select whatever webcam and microphone you want to use. Then click the Ready! button.

ai-training.glitch.me wants to connect to a serial port

Communications Port (COM1) - Paired

43

Paste your Google Teachable machine model link here:

https://teachablemachine.withgoogle.com/models/[...]

Choose Camera: NexiGo N930AF FHD webcar
Choose Audio: Default - Microphone (NexiGo

Ready!

44

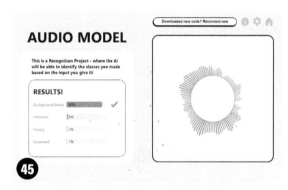

AUDIO MODEL

This is a Recognition Project - where the AI will be able to identify the classes you made based on the input you give it!

RESULTS!

Background Noise   90%   ✓
Inhaling   5%
Happy   2%
Surprised   1%

Downloaded new code? Reconnect now

45

And now you're ready to play. Since we're using an Audio Project in this chapter, you can see a helpful visualizer on screen that morphs to show your voice pattern (Figure **45**).

3. On the left, you can see all the different classes you trained, and depending on the noises in the room, you may see the little bars moving. This is the AI trying to identify what

it's hearing by comparing it to all that data you gave it. Try testing out a few of your phrases! You can see the bars change as the AI is thinking, and you'll also see a celebration on-screen when it makes a choice (Figure **46**).

Did it work? Can you see the face change on the micro:bit? The AI is always listening for changes, so if it was able to identify a class, it should have sent that class name over to the micro:bit — and assuming our code is correct, it should have activated whatever action that you placed in there.

If it didn't work, or it seems to be working only a little bit, try adjusting the Inputs tolerance bar. You can find this bar by clicking on the Open Settings gear icon on the top right (Figure **47**).

Decreasing the bar will enable the AI to choose a class without being 100% certain of what it hears. This is like telling the AI to take more chances with its guesses.

There's also a helpful Message Log window that will tell you what the AI is sending over to the micro:bit (Figure **48**).

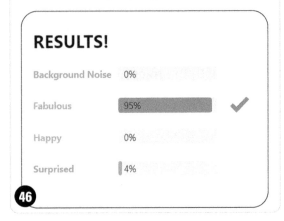

This is a Recognition Project - where the AI will be able to identify the classes you made based on the input you give it!

RESULTS!

Background Noise 0%

Fabulous 95% ✓

Happy 0%

Surprised 4%

46

Surprised | 1%

Inputs ❓ 50%

This bar here helps the AI decide how sure it is in its prediction. Crank the bar all the way up if you want it to be absolutely sure of its decision, or slide it halfway for the AI to reach a decision quicker.

47

OPEN MESSAGE LOG

9:57:30 PM Microbit Connected

9:57:35 PM AI sent Background Noise to the Microbit

9:57:53 PM AI sent Surprised to the Microbit

48

If you don't see any messages reading "AI predicted. . . ," then you need to adjust the tolerance bar or retrain your AI with even more data.

If it does read, "AI predicted . . ." but your micro:bit hasn't done anything, make sure you're still paired with the website. Repeat the steps from the beginning of this section, and then check your code for any errors.

With a little patience and some hard work, you'll be commanding your creation in no time. Amaze your family and friends with this first step in our journey with AI. You're starting off here with some very simple coding and AI interaction just to ease into this new and exciting world. The next few projects are going to add on more interesting ways the AI can interact with us. So grab some cardboard and get ready!

TAKING IT FURTHER

Now that you've created a creature with moving wings, electric lights, a face, and changing expressions, don't stop here: Think about ways you can personalize your creature.

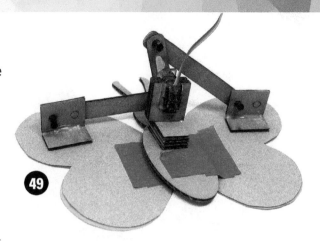

For example, redesign the body with different shapes and hinges, cover the body in pipe cleaners to give it a fuzzy feeling, or use tissue paper on the wings to give them a delicate touch. And remember: Googly eyes are *always* a fun addition to any project!

What about adding a buzzer instead of LEDs to make a bee that can buzz? Or try adding a servo motor with linkages (see page 154) to make wings that flap on their own (Figure 49).

Exploring the other blocks and drawers at the Make: AI Robots website can yield some spectacular results. Even something as simple as adding the Show String c block in the Basic Drawer gives us a way to type words or sentences that will slowly scroll across the screen. Try using one of these to make it switch back and forth between the face and words.

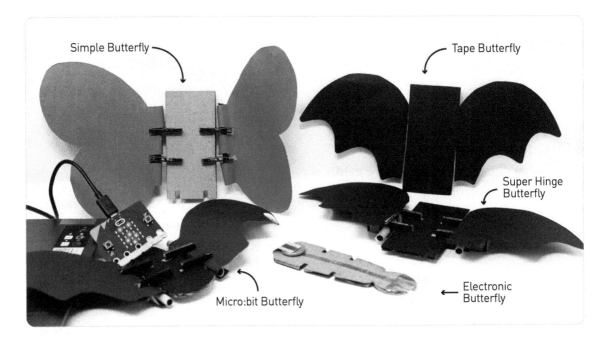

Simple Butterfly

Tape Butterfly

Super Hinge Butterfly

Micro:bit Butterfly

Electronic Butterfly

WRAPPING UP

That was a fun adventure, wasn't it? Starting with a simple cardboard cutout, we built a creature with mechanical wings, added a spark of life through LED antennae, and used a micro:bit face to show emotions. We then trained an AI to recognize words and show the appropriate expression — take a moment to congratulate yourself on a job well done!

We'll be seeing a lot of this mechanism as we continue through the other projects, so always be on the lookout for ways to improve it. When you're done tinkering with your project, head over to the next chapter where we really get things rolling!

Notes:

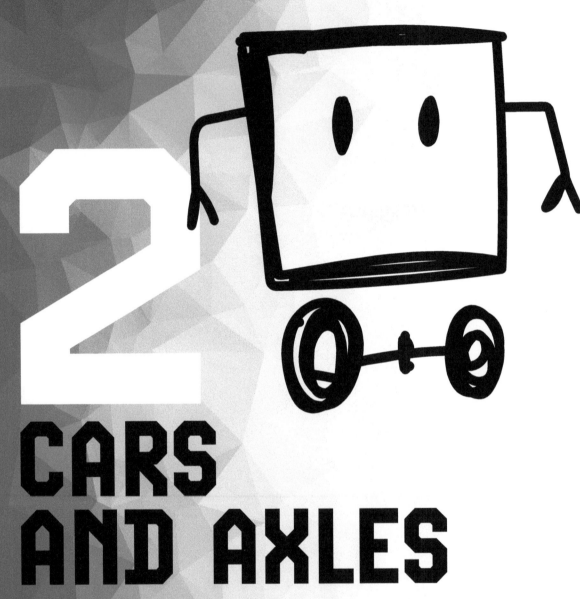

2

CARS
AND AXLES

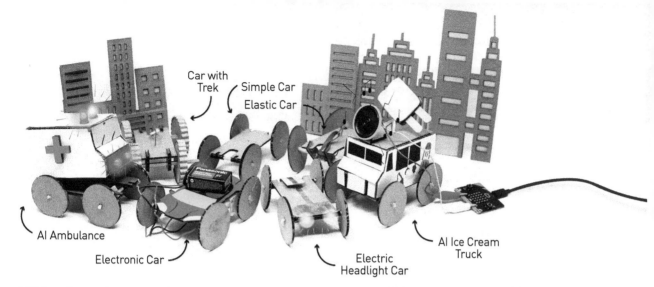

Car with Trek

Simple Car

Elastic Car

AI Ambulance

Electronic Car

Electric Headlight Car

AI Ice Cream Truck

If we're going to make more robot friends that are on the move, we should figure out a means to get from A to B smoothly. That means we'll need to talk about another simple machine that you see everyday: wheels and axles.

We're going to explore fun with wheels by building a series of cars and vehicles that become more complex the more electronics and code we add to them. You'll start out by creating a simple cardboard car with axles that enable the car to roll, then add elastic as a means of propulsion. We'll practice our new skill using copper tape to make some glowing headlights and dive into some larger motors in order to get your vehicle moving on its own. Then you'll add some micro:bit code to add some sounds, like a car horn. Finally, we'll tie all of this together by using AI to give your vehicle a mind of its own, training your AI to recognize different situations and react accordingly: Stuck in traffic? Toot your horn!

Adobe Stock-denboma

CHALLENGE CHECKLIST:

- **Build a Simple Rolling Car**
- **Add motors to power your car**
- **Code a car horn to play through a micro:bit**
- **Use AI to teach your car to react to its surroundings**

YOU WILL NEED:

- Stencils*
- Straws
- Chopstick or wooden dowel
- Axle Holders (optional)*

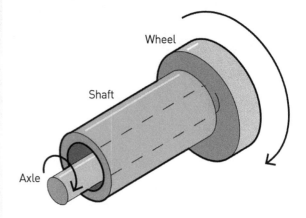

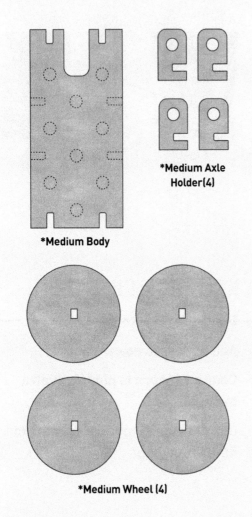

*Medium Axle Holder(4)

*Medium Body

*Medium Wheel (4)

*Download full-size PDF at
makeairobots.com/chapter2.

The most obvious place you've seen a wheel is on a car or a bike, but you may not have noticed its **axle**, the rod or shaft that connects to the wheel that enables it to rotate. These machines are all around us: They're used in a fan so the blades can spin, and even in a doorknob so it can turn to open the door. While the "wheel" part may not look like what you typically imagine, both mechanisms use hidden axles to enable rotation. For the robots you're about to make, these axles will join two wheels together, allowing them to spin at the same time.

But how can we connect this axle to our car and have it still spin? If the axle won't spin, that means the wheels won't spin, and then we'll have a car-shaped pile of cardboard. So we need a shaft, or hollow cylinder, to hold the axle while it spins. A

drinking straw can serve as our shaft if it's big enough to easily fit your axle inside, but you can also use the Axle Holder pieces from the Stencil Library instead.

The first car we're going to make relies on **contact force** to move — that's a fancy way of saying you push it yourself. Then we're going to show you a fun way to give this vehicle some independent movement by adding nothing more than a paper clip and a rubber band.

SIMPLE ROLLING CAR

1. Start by tracing the stencils onto paper, then glue them onto cardboard and cut them out.

2. If you're using a straw for the shaft, cut it into two pieces the same length as the width of the Medium Body piece. Then carefully glue a shaft near the front of the underside of your car and another near the back.

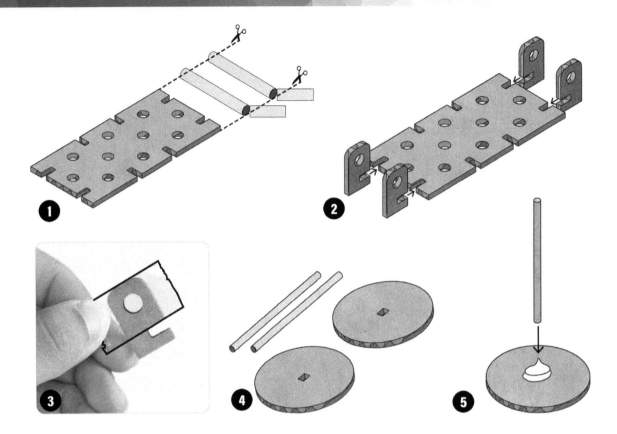

If you don't have a straw, you can alternatively attach the Axle Holders into the slots in the Medium Body piece and secure them in place with some tape or glue (Figures ❶ through ❸).

3. Now it's time to attach your axles to your wheels: Poke your chopstick or wooden dowel through the center of a wheel, and use a bit of glue to secure it in place (Figures ❹ and ❺). Once the glue dries, the axle and wheel should spin as one piece.

4. Thread this axle through the straw (or Axle Holders), and make sure your axle can turn smoothly in the shaft before gluing another wheel on the other side.

Repeat for the other set of car wheels (Figures ❻ and ❼).

And that's it (Figure ❽)! You can use some **applied force** to make the care move — your push is the source of energy to move it. Give your car a little push to see how it rolls!

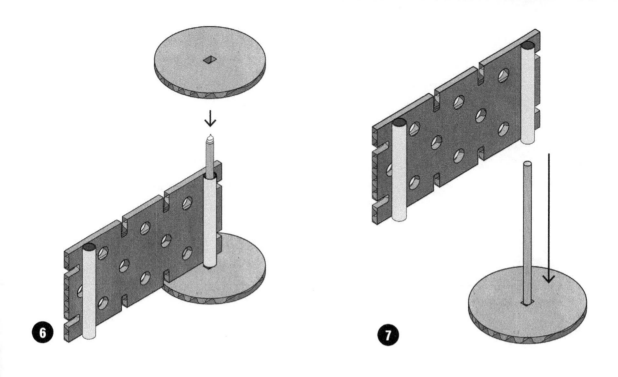

6

7

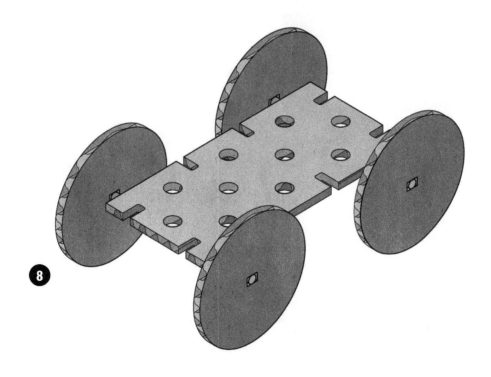

8

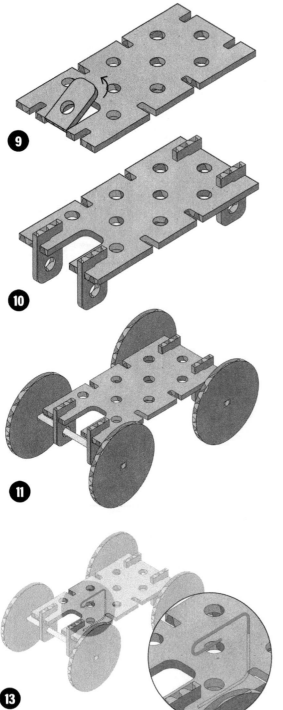

TAKING IT FURTHER

Try using a rubber band to add **spring force** — the energy released when a compressed spring returns to its normal form — as its power source: Build another car using the Axle Holders (Figures **9** through **11**), but cut a notch into the body to expose the axle. Poke a bent paper clip through the top of the body (Figures **12** and **13**), and secure it by bending it underneath and adding glue (Figure **14**).

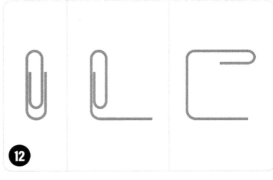

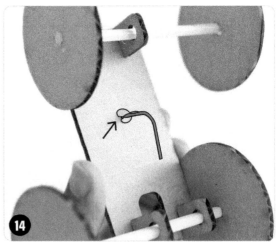

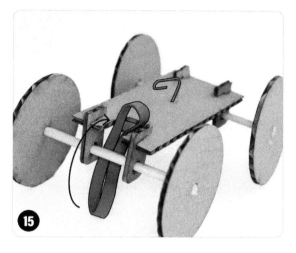

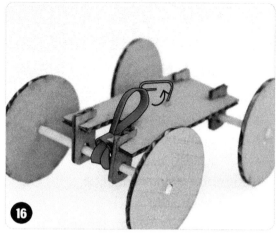

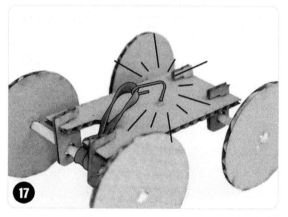

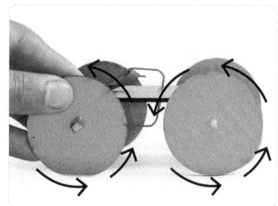

Tie one end of the rubber band around the axle (Figure **15**), and then hook the other end to the paper clip (Figures **16** and **17**). Pull the car back, and the rubber band should wrap around the axle and stretch, building up **potential energy** that powers your car upon release.

ELECTRONICS

YOU WILL NEED:

- Stencils*
- Geared DC motors (2)
- Wires
- Wire cutters or scissors
- Battery (9 V and connector recommended)
- Glue (hot glue recommended)

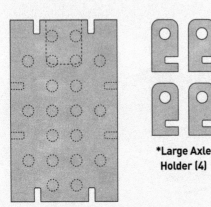

*Large Axle Holder (4)

*Large Body

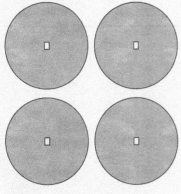

*Large Wheel (4)

*Download full-size PDF at
makeairobots.com/chapter2.

MOTOR CAR

Rubber band–powered cars are cool, but motor-powered cars are *really* cool. These small 130-size DC motors we're using are some of the more common items you'll find on your maker journey. Inside the yellow plastic housing are gears that turn another axle, the small white bump on the side. These motors work by creating a tiny magnetic current inside that rotates the central axle, which is connected to gears that turn a perpendicular axle on the motor's side. The neat thing about this magnetic current is that you can easily change the direction of the spin by changing the flow of energy through it — so if you flip your battery connections around, the motor will spin in reverse!

Before you start gluing these motors onto your car, make sure they are prepped and ready to use:

- Make sure they have secure wires coming from the front of each motor. If not, connect a wire to each of the metal prongs that stick off the silver part.
- Test the motors with a battery to make sure they work — nothing is worse than completing a project and then finding out a part is broken! Hook your wires up to

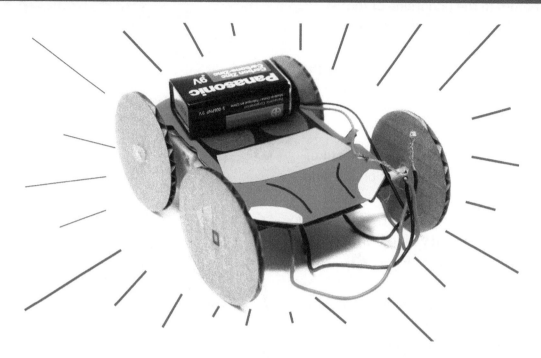

the positive and negative terminals on a 9 V battery and see if they start spinning. If not, check your wire connections to make sure they're connected to each motor (Figures **18** and **19**).

18

When your motors spin to life, you're all set to get your car body prepared. Look in the Stencil Library for the Large Body and Large Axle Holders. These will be the bones of your car to which we will attach the motors. (We're using a larger body than for the previous cars because these motors need a bit more space.)

19

1. After assembling your Large Body car, your first task is to attach the two motors to the underside of the vehicle. Make sure the little white axle bumps on the motors are pointed outward, and then secure the motors to the car body (Figure **20**). (Hot glue is best for this.)

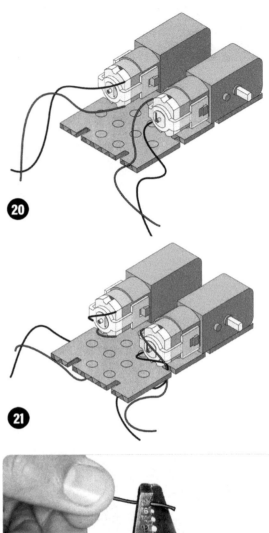

2. Now to hide those pesky wires out of the way: Cut a little notch on the side of your car body to pull the wires through to the top side. This way, they won't get tangled with the wheels or drag on the ground (Figure **21**).

3. You may want to get an adult for some help or supervision for this part: You need to connect some of these wires, so power can run from the battery into both motors. This means you'll need to use scissors or wire cutters to cut the plastic off the ends to expose the copper strands inside.

Wire cutters are the best tool for this because they have premeasured holes that cut only the plastic insulation, leaving the copper wire intact (Figures **22** and **23**). If you don't have wire cutters, you can use scissors to carefully cut into the plastic until it weakens enough to slide off without cutting through the copper wire.

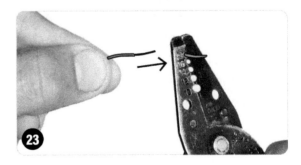

4. With all four wires from both motors exposed, now you need to connect them in a specific way: Take a red wire from one motor and a black wire from the other motor, and twist the two wires together (Figure **24**).

   Make sure you do this tightly so it looks like they've become one wire.

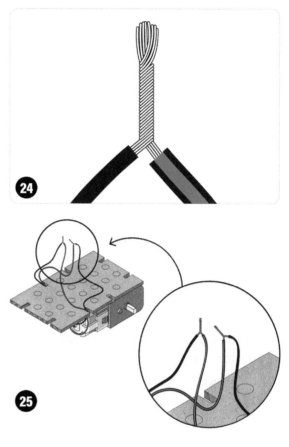

24

5. Do the same with the remaining red wire from one motor and the remaining black wire from the other motor. We should now have two sets of wires to connect to the battery, made from one red wire and one black wire from each motor (Figure **25**).

25

6. The last task is to connect those grouped wires to the battery, one set to the positive end and the other set to the negative end.

   Remember that changing the flow of current through these motors will change their direction, so if your motors are spinning in the wrong direction, simply connect the wire sets to the opposite battery ends.

26

7. Test your wires first. When you've made your choice as to which direction you want the motors to spin, connect your battery pack to the new grouped wires (Figure **26**), and this time add some tape to each connection to make sure it's really secure.

How you choose to power your vehicle is up to you. We recommend using a 9 V battery, as it will give your car the most zip, but different motors spin at different speeds, so you may prefer a lower-voltage battery, like a 1.5 V AA or AAA battery, to really slow it down.

8. Finish up by adding the other axle and wheels to your car, which will spin freely. Most real cars operate similarly, where one set of wheels are connected to the motor, and the other set just rolls. All-wheel-drive and four-whee-drive vehicles have both sets of wheels connected to the motor but require them to rotate at the same speed.

In our example, we use the Large Axle Holders from the Stencil Library to hold up the wheels to make them even with the motors, but you can also design your car to use a straw as its shaft. Experiment with other methods to see the different types of cars you can make.

TAKING IT FURTHER

You can add lights to your Motor Car in the same way you did it with chapter 1's winged creature: Use copper tape to create a simple circuit with a battery and LED headlights. Remember to make sure the LED legs are connected to the proper side of the battery — unlike with the motor, the flow of electricity for lights can go in only one direction and cannot be reversed.

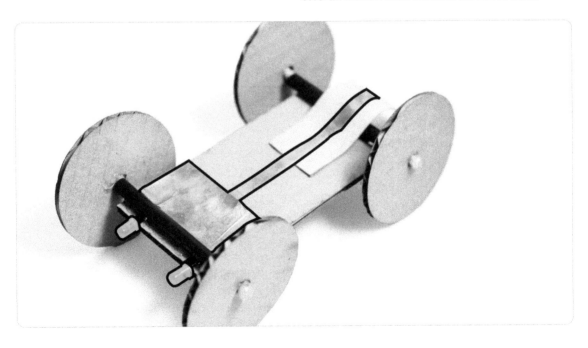

MICRO:BIT

YOU WILL NEED:

- Computer with internet access
- Micro:bit and USB cable
- One of your car projects

If your micro:bit does not have a built-in speaker, you will also need (see page 44):

- Small speaker or wired headphone with auxiliary, or aux, cable
- Wires with alligator clips

Find starter and finished micro:bit code for guidance at: makeairobots.com/chapter2

CODE LIBRARY

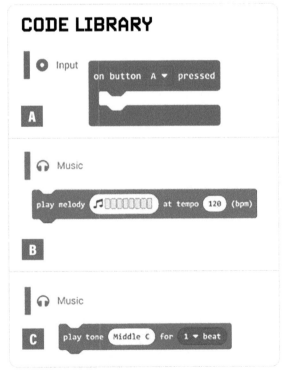

In just a few short projects, we've gone from a basic cardboard car that you needed to push along its way to a motorized machine that can speed around your workspace. But should we be worried about other cars and obstacles that may get in the way? How can our car get the attention of other "drivers"? Real cars toot a horn, and so can we!

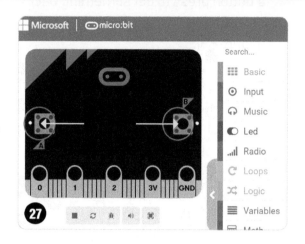

First we'll learn how code blocks can be used to create sounds (and music!), and then our project will teach you how to program our micro:bit to make a specific sound whenever we press its button — like a car horn.

Just like with our last coding project, we're going to head over to makecode .microbit.org, where we will build our code. Create a new project, and give it a name — like Cars.

1. You should see the On Start and Forever code mouths on your screen. Throw them away! (Dragging them into the left-hand column of code drawers will delete them.) If you put code blocks for sound in one of those

two code mouths, your sound will play without you doing anything; we want control over the sounds for this project, and we can get that by using the buttons on the front of the micro:bit (Figure **27**).

2. To add a button, look in the second drawer, labeled Input. You can see, sitting at the top, the code mouth named On Button [A] Pressed **A**. Drag that block onto your workspace.

    After you upload your code to the micro:bit, any code put inside this block will be activated whenever you press the micro:bit's physical A button.

    An input is how this microcontroller

will receive information from the outside world — in our case, we input a button press to get something back: an **output** in the form of sounds (Figure **28**).

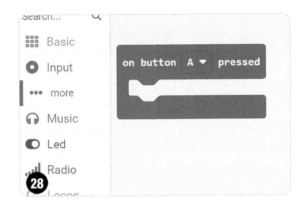

3. But what sounds can you play? Well, MakeCode gives us a ton of options to choose from in the Music drawer. The top block in this drawer is Play Melody **B** — which is like the tune of a song. Drag this block into the Button Press code block you just placed — if you click on the empty bars in the middle, you can write a little song.

   Each vertical column can play one musical note, with the column's top box producing the highest tone and each descending box producing a lower tone.

   There are eight columns that play their notes in sequence, and then repeats (Figure **29**).

4. At the top of the Play Melody block, you'll notice you're in Editor mode. If you click on Gallery, it will switch to a library of previously created songs to choose (Figure **30**).

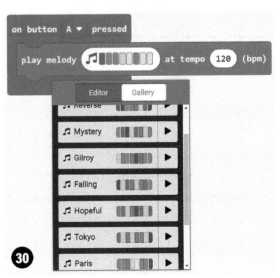

5. Now that we understand how code blocks can be used to create sound, we'll create our car horn. Delete the Play Melody code block, and replace it with the Play Tone [Middle C] for 1 Beat C block from the Music drawer. This block enables you to play a single note for one beat.

If you click on the green triangular play button on the website's virtual micro:bit (to the left of the code drawers), it'll activate your virtual code and turn from black and white into color. Press the virtual micro:bit's A Button, and you should hear it "beep" once.

Going back to your code blocks, you can click on the Middle C bubble and bring up a piano keyboard, where you can choose a different note to play. Clicking the Beat bubble will enable you to choose how long the note plays.

Now you can download your code and test the car horn. If you forgot the process, look back into chapter 1's micro:bit section (see page 13) for a refresher (Figure **31**).

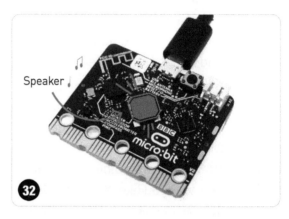

Speaker

6. You may have a newer micro:bit that has a speaker already built into it. If so, you can push the A button on your micro:bit and hear your sounds right away (Figure **32**)!

7. If you have an older micro:bit like the one featured in this book, you'll have to follow these extra steps to attach a speaker or headphone that has a little metal plug on what's called an auxiliary, or aux, cable at one end to produce your sounds.

Using a wire with alligator clips on each end, attach one of the alligator clips to the tip of the metal plug on the aux cable (Figure **33**), and connect the other end of that wire to pin 0 on the micro:bit (Figure **34**).

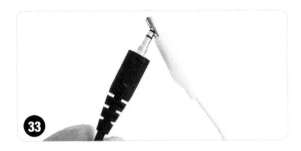

8. With the other wire with alligator clips on both ends, attach one alligator clip near the base of the plug, and connect the other end to the GND hole (Figures **35** and **36**).

That's it! You should now be able to press the A button to toot your car horn. It's up to you to attach your micro:bit onto your project in any way you like. You can add it to one of the cars we've already made, or design a new one to add to your fleet.

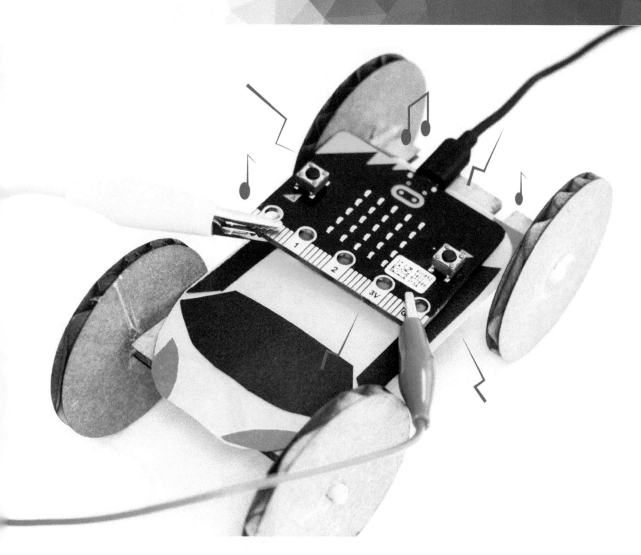

TAKING IT FURTHER

With three input buttons, A button, B button, and A+B buttons, you can control more than just a basic car horn. Create sounds and assign them to the B button and A+B buttons: Add a friendly "beep-beep" sound for when a single, low-toned beep sounds too grumpy; add a song from the music library to play, like a fancy musical horn; or compose your own song as if it's coming from a tiny car radio!

AI

YOU WILL NEED:
- Micro:bit and USB cable
- Computer with internet access
- Digital camera
- Webcam with a long USB cable

For links to the AI tools, explore resources at:
makeairobots.com/chapter2

When we're talking about AI, we want to remember why people should use it. One of its central uses is that it can organize data to help us make decisions based on that information. Since we're playing around with cars that make noise, let's create a vehicle that can choose what noise to play based on what it sees.

We should start with a model of the most important vehicle in any city, one that everybody knows and is a hero in our communities: the ice cream truck!

Grab some cardboard and have some fun with your artistic skills to create your Ice Cream Truck. When you use your imagination to create new things, there's never a wrong way to put them together. Maybe your adult helper has some suggestions, too! Work together to see what you can come up with, and let's jump into teaching our AI.

Image Project

Teach based on images, from files or your webcam.

THE TRAINING

Think of some scenarios where your Ice Cream Truck will need to play various sounds: What if it can't get where it's going? When does it turn its theme music on? Can it play different types of songs for different holidays like Halloween or winter celebrations?

Before we can code the micro:bit to react to these situations, we first have to teach our AI to identify what they are. It will do that visually, so go to the Teachable Machine website and create a new Image Project.

1. As with the AI project in chapter 1 (see page 16), we need to first provide samples of the basic scene so the AI

can learn what "nothing" looks like. Name your first class Background and take at least 20 photos to teach the AI what your empty scene looks like. We've made ours to look like a city, but yours may be your bedroom or your kitchen table (Figure **37**).

2. With that out of the way, you can start training the AI to recognize each unique situation. Start with teaching the truck to honk its horn every time it's blocked by objects, or in a traffic jam, by training it with lots of pictures of things in the way: boxes, stuffed animals, cereal bowls, other cars, or anything you have available. Let's call this class Blocked and add lots of photo data showing the AI what those obstacles look like (Figure 38).

3. The next class will help your AI decide when our truck will play its theme song. Create a class named Theme and take sample photos. This should be pretty simple — the theme music should play whenever the truck/camera sees a person, so you can train a new class that contains a bunch of photos with people or toy figures standing in front (Figure 39).

   You need lots of different photos for each of these classes to give your AI enough info to learn the difference between customers (people) and obstacles. Make sure to move your objects around in the photos to provide different angles for data.

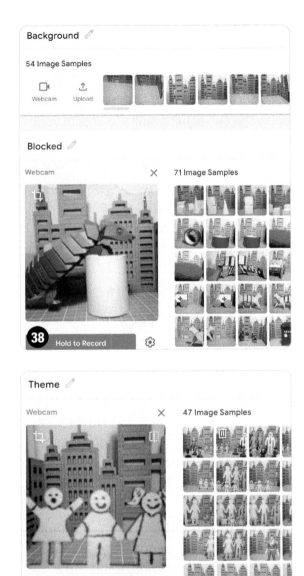

4. In addition to playing its theme music for a customer, let's have our Ice Cream Truck play special music for special things: If the Ice Cream Truck sees Halloween-y things like jack-o'-lanterns, skeletons, black cats, or witch hats, we'll have it play spooky music.

Create a Spooky class and add photos of spooky objects. They don't have to be an actual black cat, or even a toy black cat: a drawing of a black cat will work — they just need to be the same thing that the Ice Cream Truck will see.

Or pick your own theme for a class: Holidays? UFOs? Each additional song will need to be its own class, and you'll need a bunch of photos of different items from each theme to make the AI smart enough to correctly identify which theme it sees (Figure **40**).

Can you think of any other sounds or situations to which your Ice Cream Truck can react? You can add as many as you want — just remember you're going to have to code the micro:bit as well, so be prepared to add code blocks for everything you add.

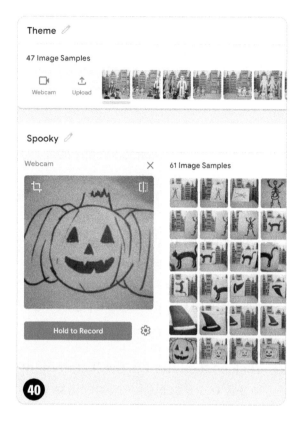

Click the Train Model button on the website when you're happy with your AI model, and remember to click Export Model (see page 18), save it to the cloud, and keep the link for use later.

THE CODE

Although we used a lot of reference photos and created multiple classes, the code for this AI project is very simple. In fact, since this AI is helping us automate the task of honking and playing music, we can use the same code that we just made in the micro:bit section. (See page 40.) With a little bit of tweaking, your workspace will sound like a bustling city street in no time at all!

1. Set up a new file on the MakeCode website called AI Car, and copy over the AI starter code from the Introduction. (See page xxxiii.)

    It's handy to create a file that already has this AI Connector Code set up and just make a copy of it every time you want to make a new AI project (Figure **41**).

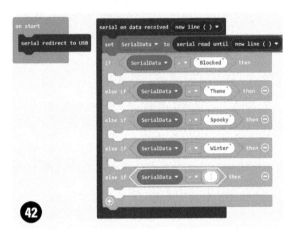

2. Click on the little + in the If statement to add more spots for each class you created (Blocked, Theme, Spooky, Winter) — and make sure you're changing the class name on each line where you see the " ". And remember to watch your spelling; this code is looking for exactly what we typed into Teachable Machine website; otherwise it won't activate the code.

    Your truck does nothing for our initial Background class when it sees an empty street, so you don't need to code anything for that — unless you want to add a truck driving sound (Figure **42**)? (Hmm, that could be fun.)

3. And now you just have to choose the sounds and songs for each class. Look back at the Micro:bit section (see page 40) for reminders on how to choose notes for a horn or how to use the Play Melody **B** block to create different songs (Figures **43** and **44**).

Downloading this code to your micro:bit (see page 13) is the last step you need to take before everything is ready. Set up your city scene in front of your webcam, and head on over to the Make: AI Robots website to start.

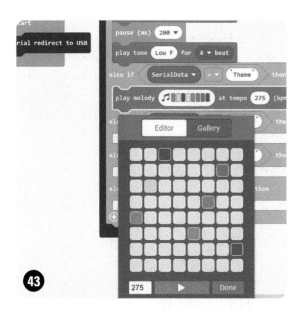

43

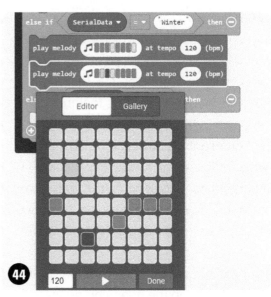

44

BRINGING IT TO LIFE

Now that the training and coding are done, we can finally sit back and enjoy some fun creation automation.

Copy and paste the link from the Teachable Machine website that has all your AI class data to the Make: AI Robots website, and it will take you to the main project page, which has all the classes that you trained it to recognize (Figures 45 and 46).

Click on the gear icon at the top right of the web page to open the Settings menu, and make sure each class is set to an "always listening" project; this ensures that your AI will tell the micro:bit to react to each new situation it sees through the webcam, instead of just the first.

Move your webcam around your city, and pause in front of the objects you added.

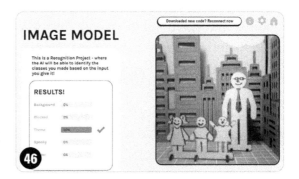

45

46

If the image on the screen is similar to any of the classes on which you trained your AI, you'll see the predictions off to the side jump around on the Teachable Machine website. The AI is looking for images similar to those you've taught it. Test different scenarios in front of your webcam to see how well your truck reacts: Does it honk when the webcam is blocked? Play its theme music for people? Play spooky music at jack-o'-lanterns?

If your AI has a hard time recognizing the objects, click on the gear icon again and adjust how easily the AI makes a decision, like you did in Chapter 1 (Figure 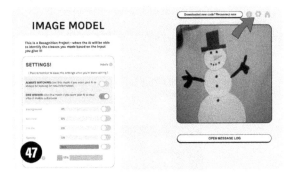). (See page 22.)

TAKING IT FURTHER

Still curious about new ways to jazz up your vehicle? A clever way to give your car some more grip against the ground is to use a bit of cardboard to create treads. If you take a strip of cardboard and pull it apart, you'll end up with a bumpy, yet bendable, strip. Glue a couple of wheels together and surround them with this new tread material to enable your car to crawl over difficult terrain (Figures 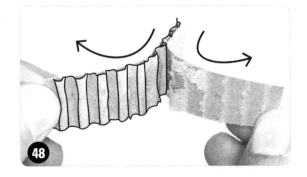 and ).

Tired of LED lights? Switch them out with a buzzer instead to give your car a horn without a micro:bit's help.

And remember, your micro:bit still has other buttons that you could use. Challenge yourself to activate something else that happens when you press the B button, or even when both buttons are pressed at the same time — you really have *three* button inputs to code sounds.

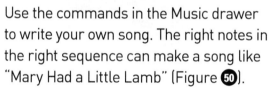

50

Use the commands in the Music drawer to write your own song. The right notes in the right sequence can make a song like "Mary Had a Little Lamb" (Figure **50**).

And with your growing confidence in making AI creations, you could even create a whole city of vehicles that can react to different situations — ambulances and fire trucks with flashing lights and sirens, construction vehicles with moving bits and sounds, or even a trolley that can stop at bus stops.

WRAPPING UP

Look at that! In just a few short lessons, you've learned the basic skills to get your robots moving: You've learned how to make wheels rotate on an axle, you've used motors for motion, and you've learned to code and to teach visual behaviors to an AI.

And you should be proud of anything that looks different from our creations — any difference is never a "mistake," but an example of you making a project your own. Whether you're using different colors, shapes, techniques, or ideas, and whether it's intentional or not, they all put your unique stamp on it. The examples in this book are just teaching examples, and we hope you apply your new skills in weird and wonderful ways!

Notes:

3

BALL
TOSS

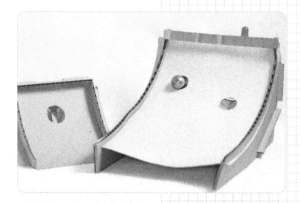

After all that hard work crafting critters and cars, let's take a break and play a game — of course, we'll have to build it first!

Much like in the bowling games you may have seen in an arcade, the goal of our game is to roll a ball up a ramp and into a hole to score points. All we need is a little cardboard and glue, some metal ball bearings, and gravity!

Adobe Stock- Jessica

We'll start with a small cardboard version with a single hole, working with regular and thin cardboard to sculpt the frame. Next, we'll add copper tape to activate an LED or buzzer when a point is scored, to add some excitement. Then we'll add a target with areas with different point values, which complicates keeping score — so we'll use the micro:bit to keep score for us! Finally, we'll make this a true arcade game by requiring coins to play, using AI to recognize different types of coins and run only when the correct amount has been inserted.

So start collecting your quarters — your arcade will soon be open for business!

CHALLENGE CHECKLIST:

- **Make a small table-top ball game**
- **Add lights or sounds**
- **Create a scoreboard with micro:bit**
- **Teach our AI to start the game when we add a quarter**

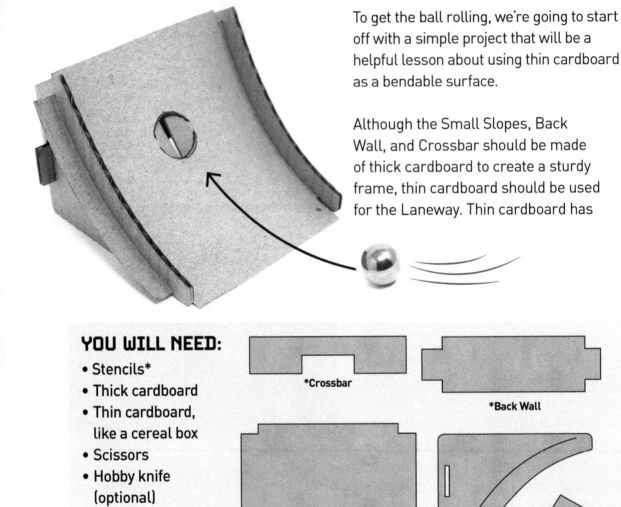

To get the ball rolling, we're going to start off with a simple project that will be a helpful lesson about using thin cardboard as a bendable surface.

Although the Small Slopes, Back Wall, and Crossbar should be made of thick cardboard to create a sturdy frame, thin cardboard should be used for the Laneway. Thin cardboard has

YOU WILL NEED:

- Stencils*
- Thick cardboard
- Thin cardboard, like a cereal box
- Scissors
- Hobby knife (optional)
- Glue/hot glue
- Metal ball bearing

*Crossbar

*Back Wall

*Hinge Hole

*Laneway

*Small Slope (2)

*Download the full-size PDF at makeairobots.com/chapter3.

more rigidity than regular paper, but won't bend at a sharp angle like thick cardboard. A ramp made of thin cardboard can provide the gentle curve that this project needs.

BALL TOSS GAME

1. Begin by tracing the Laneway stencil onto a thin piece of cardboard, and cut it out (Figure ❶).

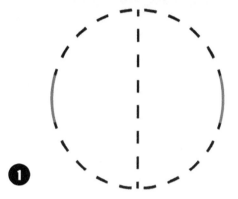

    Determine where you'd like your target, draw it on the Laneway, and cut it out. If you just want a simple hole in your cardboard, anything about the size of a quarter will be fine (Figure ❷).

    You can also use the Hinge Hole stencil to make the Hinged Doors that we'll be using later in the Electronics section. A thin hobby knife is the best tool for precise cuts, but it's *very sharp and may require adult help*. Make sure to cut only the dotted lines, and *do not cut the red lines* — that part will fold back and serve as hinges (Figure ❸).

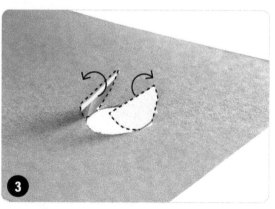

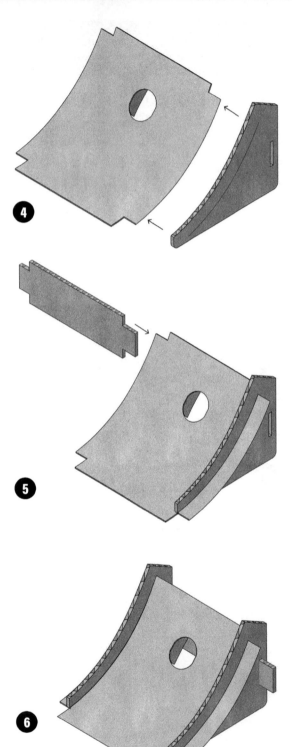

2. After you cut out the Small Slope wall pieces, cut along the dotted line on both Small Slopes to make a slot big enough to slide in the thin cardboard Laneway. The Laneway should stick through the slot about half an inch (Figure ❹).

3. Cut out the Back Wall, and cut slots into the back of both Small Slope walls. Unlike the slits for the thin cardboard Laneway, the slots for the Back Wall must be wider to accommodate the Back Wall's thicker cardboard. Insert the Back Wall into the slots to help keep both of the Small Slope walls spaced apart from each other (Figure ❺).

4. Attach the other Small Slope wall, making sure both the Back Wall and the Laneway fit snugly into their spots (Figure ❻).

5. To prevent your marble from launching into the sky (and possibly breaking a nearby window), trace the Crossbar onto thick cardboard, cut it out, and glue it onto the top of the Small Slopes to serve as a blocker (Figure ❼).

After all the glue dries, your game is ready to play. Try to roll a metal ball bearing up

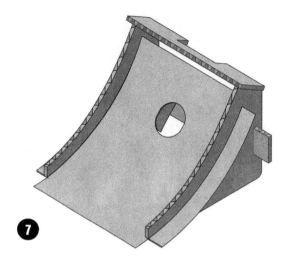

the ramp and into the hole. If you don't have a metal ball bearing, you can use something else, like a marble.

TAKING IT FURTHER

It takes a little practice to learn how much force you need to roll the ball, and how to roll it straight toward your target. If it's a little difficult to hit your target, remember that's part of the challenge! If it's too easy to hit your target, try gluing some obstacles onto the Laneway, like you would find in a pinball machine.

ELECTRONICS

YOU WILL NEED:

- Stencils*
- Thick cardboard
- Thin cardboard, like a cereal box
- Scissors
- Hobby knife
- Glue/hot glue
- Copper tape
- 1.5 V coin cell battery, like a CR2032 or CR2025
- LEDs
- Electric buzzer and connecting wires (optional)
- Metal ball bearing

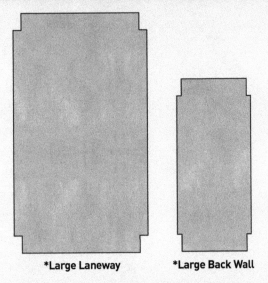

*Large Laneway   *Large Back Wall

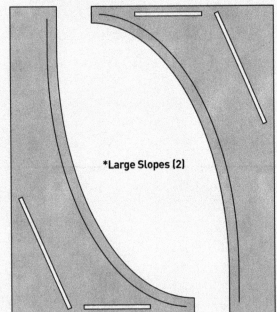

*Large Slopes (2)

*Hinge Hole

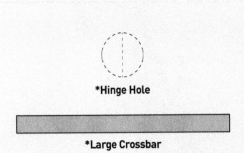

*Large Crossbar

*Download the full-size PDF at makeairobots.com/chapter3.

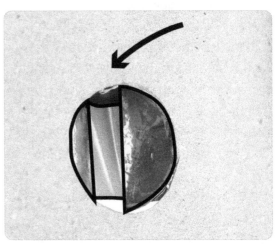

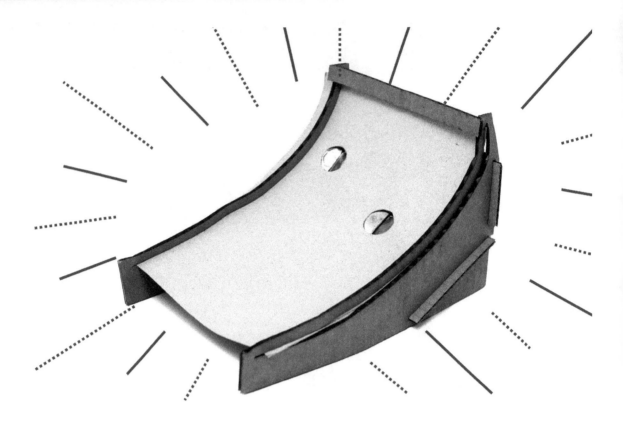

As with our previous projects, we're going to use copper tape to make a circuit. Only this time, we're going to make an open circuit, which has a gap in the circuit path so the electrical current won't flow. We'll create that gap by covering the hole doors with copper tape but pushing them slightly open — the electricity can't move through the circuit because it has no way to get across the gap between the doors.

This is why we're using a metal ball bearing. As the metal ball touches both doors on its way through the hole, the electricity can flow across the ball and briefly create a closed circuit that activates our indication light.

You may notice the ball passes through too fast to get a nice bright light from the LED. Try adding a bit of tape behind the doors to hold them closer together, creating a small cup that keeps the ball in place a little longer before dropping down.

1. After you've created the parts of your game with help from the Stencil Library, we'll start by creating the circuit on the back of the Large Laneway.

Use the Hinged Doors stencil to create two targets in the Large Laneway, and be careful not to cut the hinges. (If you accidentally cut out the whole circle, you can reattach them with regular tape.) Cover the Hinged Doors in copper tape and add copper-tape tabs to the back of the Large Laneway as contact points for building your circuit (Figure **8**).

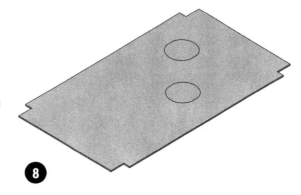

2. Make a button (see page 7) out of thin cardboard to house your coin cell battery and glue it in the center above the Hinged Doors so you can turn your game off when not in use. Remember that the negative side of the battery should sit on the copper tape covering the button's base (Figure **9**).

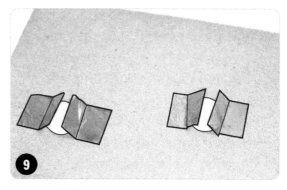

3. Now you can make some circuits. Use copper tape to branch a path from the left Hinged Door to the positive (longer) leg of the LED.

Use copper tape to branch a path from the right Hinged Door over the top of the button to the button's other side so when you fold the button down, the copper tape touches the positive side of the battery.

Finally, use copper tape to create a short path from the negative side of

the battery to the negative (shorter) leg of the LED (Figure **10**).

When the button is on and the Hinged Doors are closed and touching, the circuit should be complete and activate the LED.

(If your light doesn't turn on, remember that electricity flows in one direction and check that the negative side of the battery is connected to the negative leg of the LED and the positive side of the battery is connected to the positive leg of the LED.)

Slightly push the Hinged Doors to separate them and open the circuit.

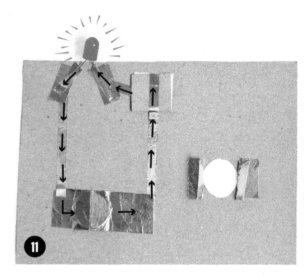

4. Now that you have one complete circuit, it's quite easy to add the other hole into this loop by branching off from the battery in the other direction. We've attached an electronic buzzer to the second target, but you can also connect another LED (Figure **11**).

(It's OK to piggyback on part of the first circuit instead of creating a completely new branch to the battery — in our example, we have a new path branching from the battery's negative side, but we're tapping into the existing path back to the positive side, essentially making two overlapping circuits.)

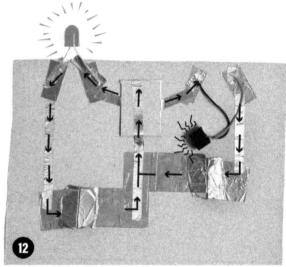

5. After the circuits are complete, test them by pushing the metal ball bearing through the Hinged Doors and seeing whether the LED lights up. You may need to adjust the doors to find an optimal starting distance apart (Figure **12**).

Assemble the game as you did with the basic game, but notice that we've added a Ball Return piece toward the bottom that fits into the second slot of the Large Slopes. This piece creates a way for your ball bearing to roll back to you after it goes through the holes so you won't have to chase after them as they roll off the table (Figure **13**)!

TAKING IT FURTHER

Try connecting something else into this circuit. We used a buzzer here for one of the holes, but you can experiment with different colored LEDs, or even a motor.

With this lesson in mind, you can create more circuits or add multiple LEDs to the same circuit; just remember that each light draws electricity, so three LEDs on the same circuit may be much dimmer than a single LED.

And your circuits don't need to run off the same battery — just be careful that the electrical paths touch where you want them to touch so they don't interfere with each other. Get creative!

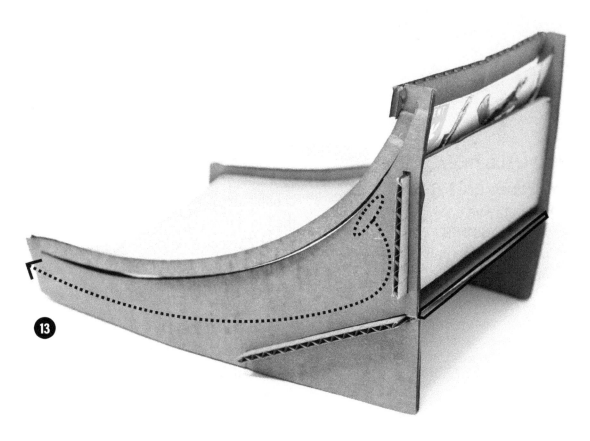

13

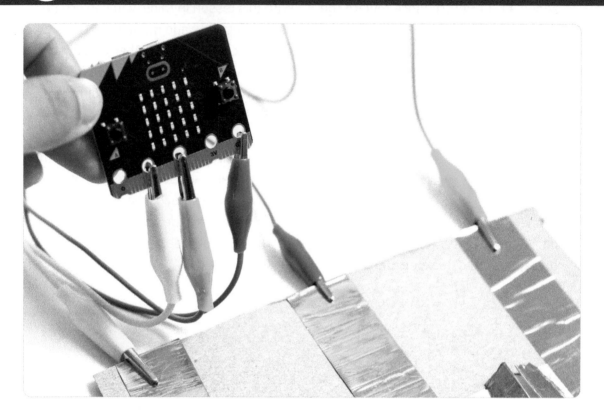

YOU WILL NEED:

- Your Large Ball Toss game
- Alligator clips
- Micro:bit and USB cable
- Computer with internet access
- Copper tape
- LED (5 mm or 10 mm)

Find starter and finished micro:bit code for guidance at: makeairobots.com/chapter3

With a few micro:bit projects under your belt, you're discovering its many capabilities. As with most technologies, the fun is thinking of creative ways to apply that tech. For instance, since we already have a complete game, why not use the mirco:bit to keep score?

This project is going to help us dive a little deeper into coding with the micro:bit by opening up a few more of those coding drawers and learning some new tricks.

CODE LIBRARY

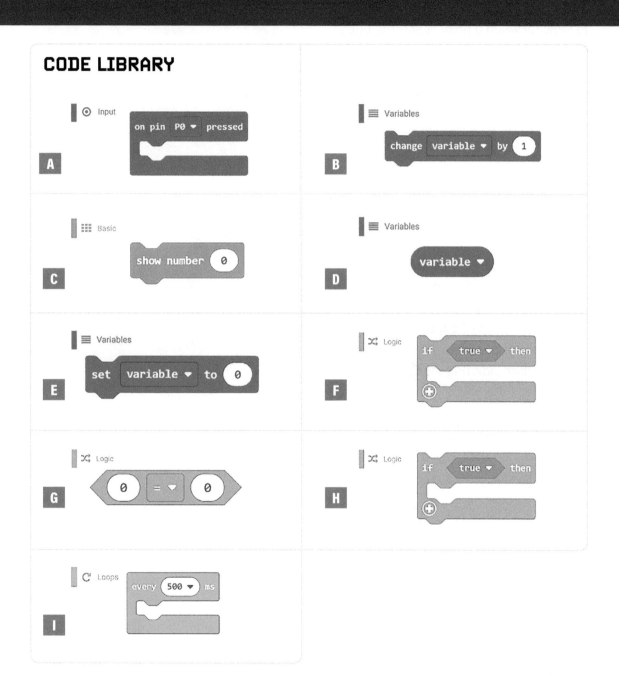

A — Input: on pin P0 ▼ pressed

B — Variables: change variable ▼ by 1

C — Basic: show number 0

D — Variables: variable ▼

E — Variables: set variable ▼ to 0

F — Logic: if true ▼ then

G — Logic: 0 = ▼ 0

H — Logic: if true ▼ then

I — Loops: every 500 ▼ ms

The large Ball Toss game we created in the Electronics section used a light to indicate when a point is scored, but we still had to keep track of the running score. In this project, we're replacing the circuit with one connected to a micro:bit that keeps the score for us.

We'll create a new Large Laneway, but you may be able to reuse other parts from our previous project, like the Large Slopes, Back Wall, and Ball Return.

1. Cut open the Hinged Doors and cover them with copper tape like in the previous project, then run straight lines of copper tape to the top of the board and slightly over to the other side (Figure **14**).

   Make sure one piece of copper tape connects both of the Hinged Doors. This will be the GND strip — a return path for our electrical current.

2. Connect an alligator clip to the middle GND strip, and connect the other end to the GND pinhole on our micro:bit (Figure **15**).

   Connect a second alligator clip between one of the other tape paths and pin 1 on the micro:bit, and then connect a third alligator clip between

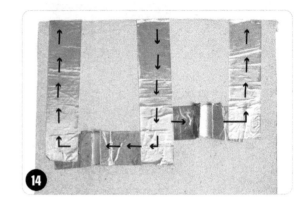

14

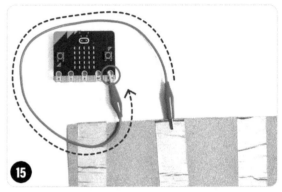

15

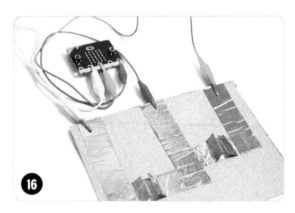

16

the remaining tape path and pin 2 on the micro:bit (Figure **16**).

And with that simple setup, our basic scoreboard is ready for coding!

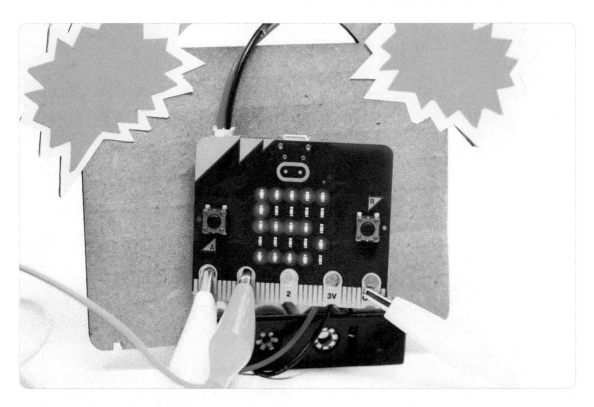

Instead of power coming from a coin cell battery, the micro:bit's USB connector outputs an electrical current from pin 1 and pin 2 that is interrupted by the open Hinged Doors.

When the ball goes through the Hinged Door holes, it will complete the circuit back to the micro:bit as an input signal.

SCOREBOARD GAME

Our first game is simple — we just want to assign each target hole a different number of points and have the micro:bit display that information. This will require us to use **variables**, or information that can be changed either by us or by the code, in order for the micro:bit to remember how many points we have. Let's see how high of a score you can get!

1. As always, start with a fresh blank page for your code, and name your project something catchy like Super Scoreboard.

2. Set up some code to enable the micro:bit to communicate with the circuits we've attached to the pin 1 and pin 2.

Opening the Input drawer, you can see the On Pin [P1] Pressed [A] code mouth. This block will activate code whenever an electrical current or signal is detected on the selected pin (Figure **17**).

Drag two of these code blocks into your workspace and set the pins in the dropdown menu — in this case pin 1 and pin 2 — where you've connected the circuits. Now whatever is added into these code mouths will be activated when the metal ball bearing connects the copper tape on the Hinged Doors.

3. Open the Figure drawer and click on the Make a Variable button (Figure **18**).

4. This variable is going to save our score, so let's name it Score.

Note: While it's fun to give things silly names, naming your variable after its function is helpful to keep you organized. When your code gets super long and there are lots of functions, easily recognizing the purpose of each variable will keep things simple.

5. Clicking on the Make a Variable button created two new items in this drawer: Set Score to (0) and Change Score by

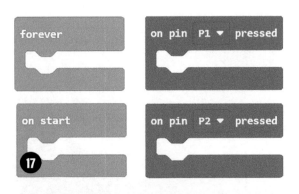

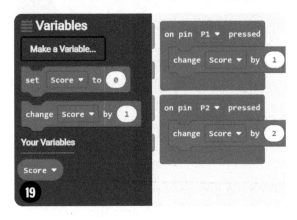

(1). Drag the Change Score by (1) [B] block into the pin 1 code mouth (Figure **19**).

By changing the number in the text field, we can set how many points we get from each target hole. Use this same block in both code mouths, but have them change the score by different amounts. If you like basketball, set a variable to one point like for a free throw and the other to two points like for a field goal (or a three-pointer?).

6. Now that the micro:bit is keeping score, let's have it display that score. One of the coolest things about the micro:bit's LED screen is that it can display numbers and letters, which means it can show our Score variable!

In the Basic drawer, drag the Show Number C block into the Forever code mouth. This command tells the micro:bit to continuously display our score on its screen (Figure ⑳).

But this code block is currently set to show a specific number, in this case 0. Open the Variable drawer again and find the small bubble block that reads Score D.

We can drag this bubble block to different spots in our code to call, or activate, our variable. Drag this bubble block over the zero and see what happens.

You can see in the preview off to the side that the screen is now showing our score of zero.

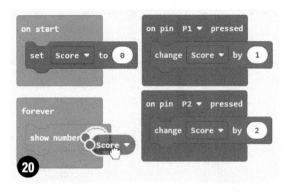

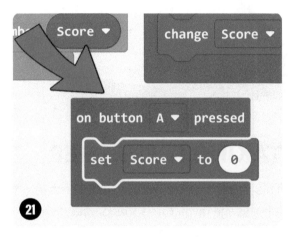

7. One last block of code we may want to add to this project will add a button to reset our score to zero. Review our previous car-horn lesson where we added a button (see page 42), and try to add a button to change the Score variable back to zero using the Set [Variable] to E block (Figure ㉑).

And there you have it! Just design a little scoreboard frame to hold your micro:bit, and you're all set to play.

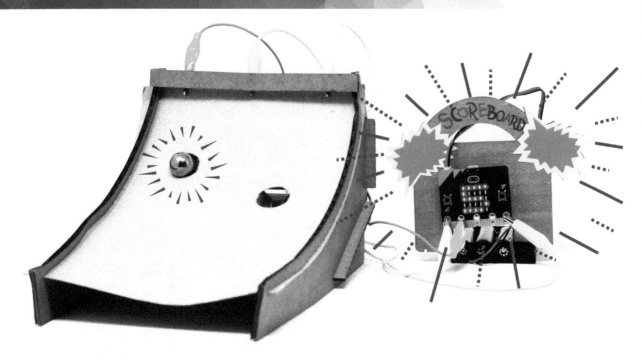

TAKING IT FURTHER

This second game enables us to create a message or pictures that display when you reach a specific score.

1. Using an If [True] Then block **F** from the Logic drawer, we can tell the code to do something when the score variable reaches a specific number. Place the If [True] Then block **F** in the Forever code mouth, because we want the code to constantly check whether the score meets our chosen condition (Figure **22**).

2. Replace the small True hexagon with one of the 0 = 0 **G** hexagons from the Logic drawer (Figure **23**).

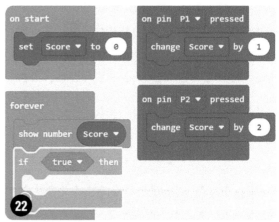

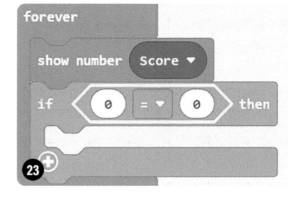

3. Now we need to change some of the information in this little block. Drag another Score bubble (from the Variable drawer) into the first spot, and change the second 0 to whatever you want the winning score to be. So if you are playing to 10 points, it would read "If Score ≥ 10 Then" (Figure ㉔).

It's important to use the > or = symbol instead of just = because your score might go beyond the winning number you set.

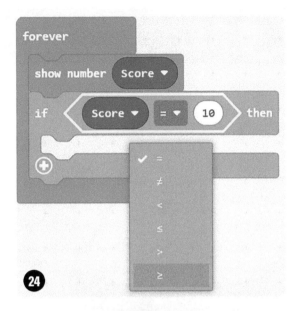

You can check how your If statement works by reading it to yourself out loud: "If our Score is greater than or equal to 10, then do this".

4. Now that the If statement is set up and looking for a specific condition to be met, anything you put in the If statement's mouth will activate when you reach the winning score: Explore the different images you can make with the LED screen, or use the Show String **H** block to have it show a message like "You Win!" (Figure ㉕).

Or what about music? If you connect a speake to pin 0, you can revisit the melody block from chapter 2 (see page 42) and see if you can find a "winning" tune.

Remember to add some code to reset your score to 0 before you can play again, perhaps connected to one of the micro:bit physical buttons.

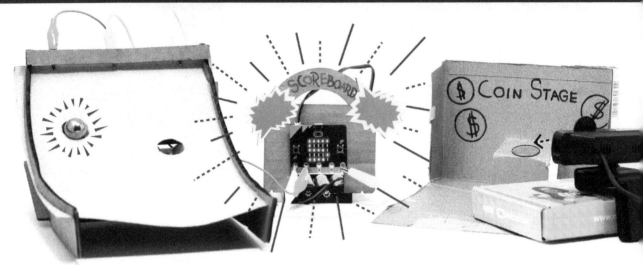

YOU WILL NEED:

- Multicircuit Ball Toss game
- Alligator clip wires
- Webcam
- Micro:bit and & USB cable
- Computer with internet access
- A quarter (or other coins)

For links to the AI tools, explore resources at:
makeairobots.com/chapter3

We now have a game to challenge our skill with a real working scoreboard and maybe some lights or music. This kind of fun is worth paying for — and we're going to enable just that.

We're going to train an AI to recognize and differentiate between coins, and write a little bit of code to tell the arcade game to activate when a player inserts a quarter.

THE TRAINING

Just as with all of our other AI projects so far, we're going to start by training the AI. Hop on over to the Teachable Machine website (see page xxix) and click on Image Project (Figure **26**).

We made a nifty little stage to place our coins on, but you can use anything — even

26

a blank piece of paper — as long as the AI can clearly see the coins through the webcam. We're going to train our AI to recognize the coin, so an uncomplicated visual background works best (Figure 27).

27

1. Make the first class our No Coin image database of what the coin stage looks like without anything on it. (See page 47 for a reminder of all the steps to create a class.) Take a bunch of photos of your coin stage with no money on it from slightly different angles so the AI knows what it looks like when no money has been added (Figure 28).

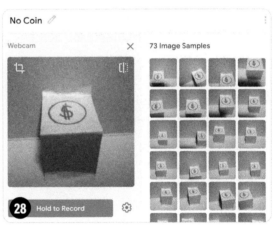

No Coin ✎

Webcam ✕   73 Image Samples

28 Hold to Record ⚙

2. Once that's complete, make a new class and call it Quarters. Put a quarter on the stage and take a bunch of pictures of it in different positions on the stage and from different angles (Figure 29).

Remember to take pictures of both sides of the quarte so it'll be recognized no matter which side is up. You need at least eight photos to move on, but the more photos you have, the smarter your AI gets.

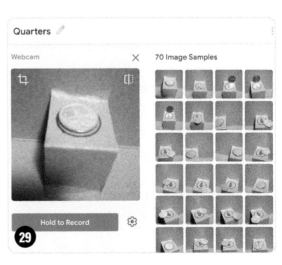

Quarters ✎

Webcam ✕   70 Image Samples

Hold to Record ⚙

29

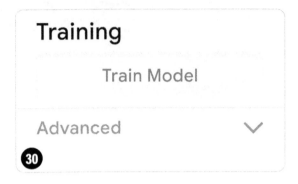

Training

Train Model

Advanced ⌄

30

31

3. You can add more types of coins — or bottle caps, cardboard discs, washers, or anything you'd like to use as a token — by creating extra classes with pictures set up the same way as you did for Quarters. Don't forget to name each class!

4. Once you're satisfied that the AI has enough data to recognize your classes, click the Train Model button, and wait a moment as your AI learns (Figure **30**).

   After a few seconds, the testing window will spring to life. If you've trained your AI to recognize different coins, make sure it can tell the difference between each coin (Figure **31**).

   When you're happy with your AI and you know it can tell a quarter from a penny, export your AI and click the Upload to Website button on the

following page. Save this link (or keep this page open) while you head over to makecode.microbit.org to code the micro:bit's reactions.

THE CODING

The AI is ready to recognize when a quarter has been put into the game, but you need to tell it what to do when that happens.

1. Let's work from the Ball Toss example we created in the previous project — a simple game that will show your score. Using the On Pin [P1] Pressed **A** code mouth, add this short program into the starter code (see page xxxiii) we use to connect to our AI website (Figure **32**).

2. If you build a simple version that is looking only for quarters, replace the text area in the If statement with the word *Quarters* ("if [SerialData] [=] ("Quarters") then") (Figure **33**).

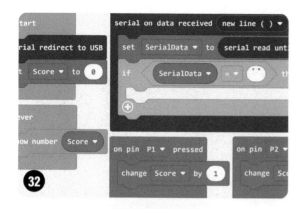

32

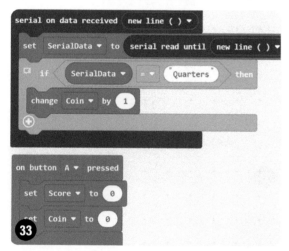

33

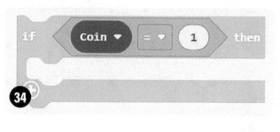

34

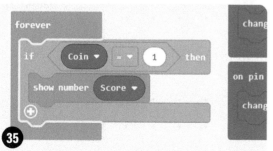

35

Make sure the spelling is exactly the same as your quarter class title on the Teachable Machine website — that's what it's looking for here.

When the AI now recognizes a quarter through the webcam, it's ready to do something. Create a new Variable called Coin, and add a new block inside this If statement that uses Change [Coin] by 1 **B**.

Remember to create a Set [Coin] to 0 in your On Start block so the coin count always starts at zero.

3. Now you need to instruct the code to run whenever it knows that Coin = 1. Build another If Statement that constantly looks to see if Coin = 1 (Figure **34**).

This If statement should surround the Show Number **C** block that we have in the Forever block. This way, no numbers will appear until a quarter has been inserted — in other words, the scoreboard won't work until a player inserts a quarter (Figure **35**).

Take a quick look at the code we set up earlier for adding points. Is there anything stopping the score from increasing if no quarter has been inserted?

We need to put additional If statements around these blocks as well to prevent the score from being changed before money is inserted.

Last, after you reset your score to zero, add a Set [Coin] to 0 **E** block. When the game restarts with the scoreboard cleared, it will "use" a coin credit and require another coin for the next game (Figure **36**).

Now upload your code to the micro:bit, and we're ready to see how it all comes together.

BRINGING IT TO LIFE

And now it's time to dig into your piggy banks to finally see how well the game works. Go to the Make: AI Robots website and copy and paste the code that the Teachable Machine website gave us. This will open up a project page that runs similar to the Ice Cream Truck project from chapter 2 (Figure **37**).

Set up your coin stage in front of your webcam and hit the Start button. If you trained everything properly, it shouldn't detect any coins on the blank stage, and your game won't work at all. Now add a quarter to the stage, and amaze your friends and family with your coin-operated arcade game (Figure **38**)!

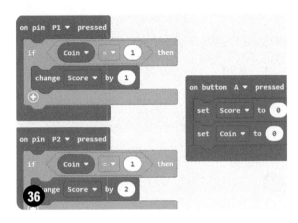

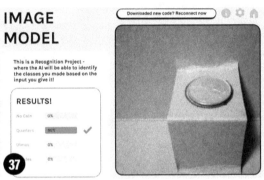

TAKING IT FURTHER

This chapter's project has a lot of potential for creative ways to enhance our game. For instance, you can use some cardboard, a rubber band, and an axle from chapter 2 to build a Popsicle stick "kicker" to launch your ball (Figures 39) and 40).

Or instead of a light, try using just a small buzzer instead; it can be attached in the same way as the LED. Now your game will make an electronic buzz every time a point is scored (Figure 41).

Or if you want to make the game more challenging, here's a way to count how long it took to get a winning score by using variables to make the micro:bit work like a clock that can keep time.

You'll need an Event **I** block from the Loops drawer, which gives us a way to repeat an action after a certain time interval. Change the number in the dropdown menu from 500 milliseconds to 1,000 milliseconds (which is one complete second), and then create a new Variable called Time and have it add one to this number every second the game is running using a Change [Time] by 1 **B** code block (Figure 42).

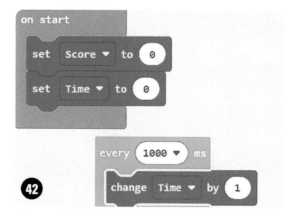

This will run in the background, but you need a way to record the time when you win; otherwise, it may have changed again before it's displayed. Use a second Variable to save the Time Variable exactly when you score the winning goal. In our example, we're playing a victory song (Figure **43**)!

You can also make a game that sees how many points you can score before a timer runs out by setting a starting time and then setting the Time Variable to –1 so it counts down.

And if you don't have quarters, you can enhance your AI by training it to recognize other coins and use code to have your micro:bit add their values together to reach 25 cents (Figure **44**).

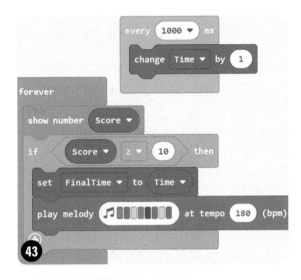

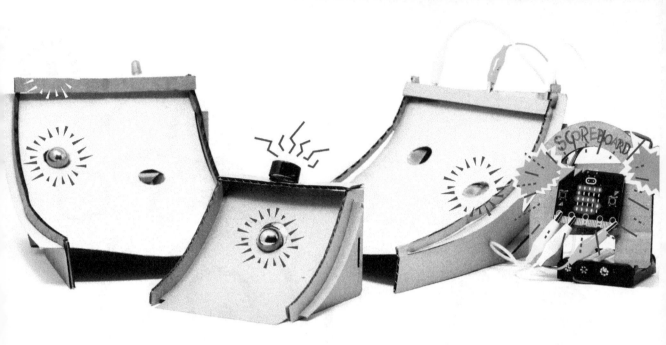

WRAPPING IT UP

After a long day of fun, even carnivals need to close down for the night. Be proud of yourself because your maker skills have improved a ton over the past few chapters. We've created increasingly complicated circuits, and have started to explore more complex code activities. If you've been trying the Taking It Further challenges, then you also have experience with more advanced code and functions now.

You're using the skills and mechanisms learned from previous chapters and building on your knowledge. Just like AI, the more you learn, the more confident you will become in your abilities and choices, enabling you to build more amazing things!

4 MARBLE RUNS!

That last game we made was a lot of fun, so let's keep the ball rolling — literally! We're going to build pieces for a Marble Run, which is a long structure on which you roll marbles down in interesting ways. As long as you have marbles, some building material, and an imagination, you're all set.

First, you're going to construct some interactive areas for the marbles as they roll, and some pathways to connect those pieces. Then you'll use your knowledge of electronics to make a section that can randomly change the path of a marble. Using the micro:bit, you'll learn how to take control of which path your marble will follow. And finally, you'll create an AI that can tell which marble crossed the finish line first and wins the race!

This chapter combines many of the maker concepts you've already learned, including hinges, axles, slopes, copper circuits, and electronics. If you felt challenged by previous chapters, this will be a great opportunity to revisit and hone your skills!

CHALLENGE CHECKLIST:

- **Design some simple sections for a Marble Run**

- **Add a motor to a new Marble Run design**

- **Use the micro:bit to change paths**

- **Train the AI to judge the winner of your Marble Run!**

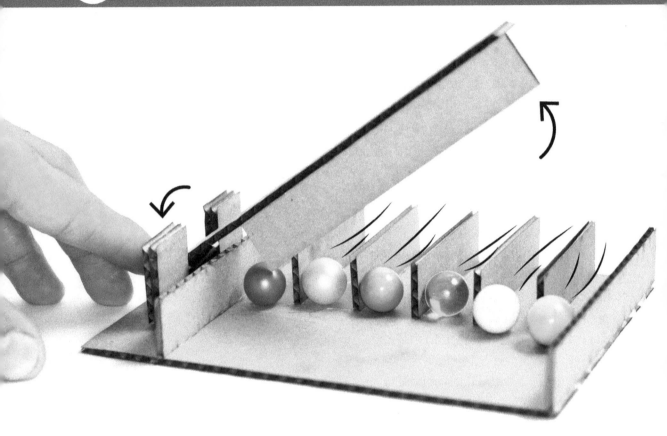

MARBLE RACE

There are so many different things we could make for our Marble Runs — we could design a way to score points at the end of the race, or spinners to help bounce things around; the possibilities are *endless*. Why don't we start at the beginning — literally?

Since we'll eventually use AI to turn this Marble Run into a Marble *Race*, we're going to create a starting gate.

To run a fair race, we'll make a device that releases all of our marbles at once. It would be easiest to build something we can just lift upward, but that would be a bit more challenging to automate later. Instead, we'll revisit **hinges** from chapter 1 as the heart of our project.

YOU WILL NEED:

- Stencils*
- Cardboard
- Scissors
- Hot glue
- Straw
- Boxes and containers to build in (optional)
- Toothpick or thin, sturdy material
- Marbles

*Wall A (4)

*Wall B (5)

*Wall D (3)

*Wall E (1)

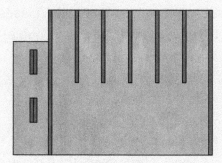

*Starting Gate

*Download the full-size PDF at makeairobots.com/chapter4.

STARTING GATE

1. With all your parts traced and cut out, take two of the Wall D pieces and use hot glue to connect them onto the edges of your platform to create the outside walls (Figures ❶ and ❷).

2. Set up the lanes for the different marble teams. Glue the five Wall B pieces onto the board, creating six evenly spaced lanes. (If you didn't trace our marking lines from the stencil, make sure your lanes are about ¾ inch apart, large enough to fit a marble (Figure ❸).

3. Glue two sets of the Wall A pieces together so you have two double-thick pieces (Figure ❹).

4. Glue these double-thick pieces vertically onto the little platform on the side of your marble lanes so they sit apart a little more than the width of the last Wall D piece (Figure ❺).

5. Cut a small length of straw that can fit between the two double-thick pieces. This will serve as our hinge and will be further secured in step 8 (Figure ❻).

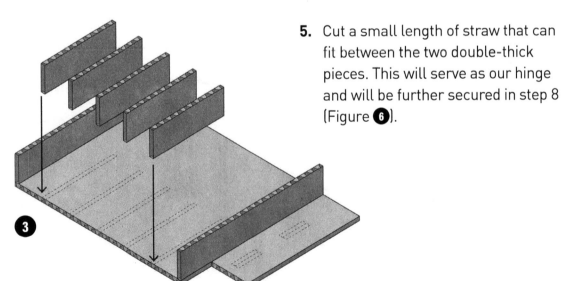

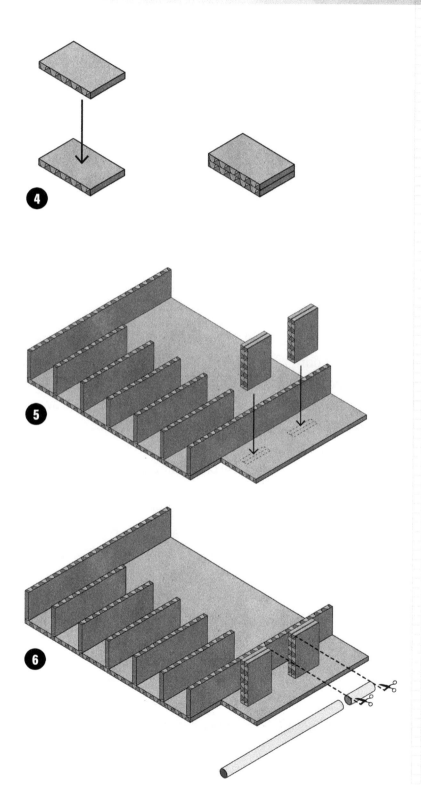

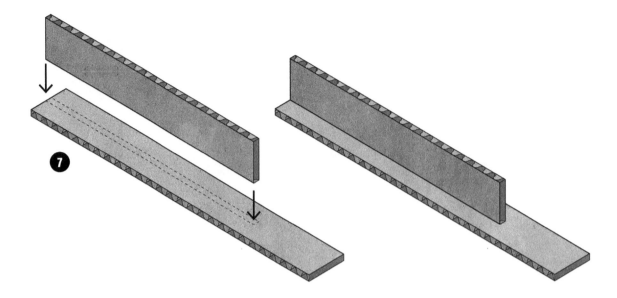

6. A Wall D piece is the perfect length to block all six lanes and prevent our marbles from rolling away, so this will be the blocker on our gate. Glue Wall D perpendicularly onto the Wall E piece, starting at one end (Figure **7**).

7. Place Wall E across the lanes — so that Wall D blocks all the lanes — but below the straw hinge.

    Measure where the gate touches the straw hinge. If placed correctly, Wall D will be blocking the lanes, and Wall E should extend beyond the double-thick Wall A pieces.

    Once Wall E is in the proper position, glue it to the straw hinge (Figures **8**).

8. Secure the hinge to the double-thick Wall A pieces by inserting a toothpick through the wavy insides of the cardboard, through the straw, and out the other side. Add some glue or tape to the ends to prevent the toothpick from sliding out (Figures **9** and **10**).

We actually just created a **lever**, a simple machine that uses a rigid beam (Wall E) attached to a pivot point (the straw hinge) to move an object (Wall D).

And there you have a super-simple Starting Gate. Add a handle or larger pad to press down on, and, maybe some flashy signs or flags, then congratulate yourself: You've just completed the first component of your Marble Run!

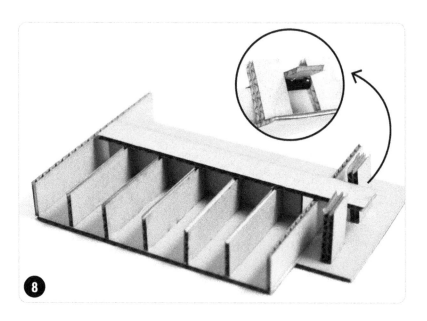

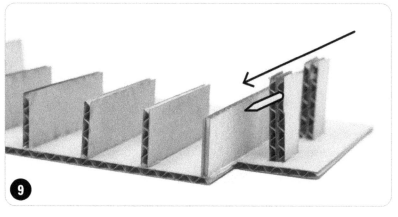

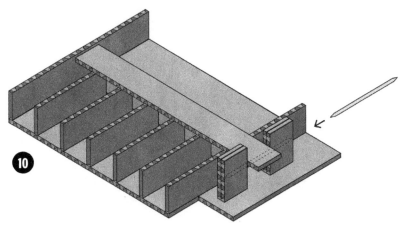

TAKING IT FURTHER

Using other recycled materials from around the house can be a great way to connect these sections and keep the balls rolling. Supplies such as milk cartons, soda bottles, and especially paper towel rolls are great because they are easy to find and cut up — just make sure that the containers are empty first!

You probably have plenty of ideas to join the sections of your Marble Run, but consider this clever way to connect your cardboard creations.

Notes:

THE SPIRAL

When you're designing paths for our marbles to follow, you may find it challenging to create a smooth track that curves in another direction. Cardboard doesn't really want to bend without creasing and folding on itself, and that makes for a bumpy ride. But try this technique to bend cardboard to your wishes:

1. Measure the length of each Spiral Road and cut two straight strips of cardboard to that length and 1 inch wide. Starting at one end of the strip, pinch one side of the cardboard and slowly peel it away from the corrugated "waves." Cut away any remaining fibers if it doesn't peel away cleanly (Figure ⑪). The cardboard strips should now be flexible without the cardboard's backing.

2. Carefully glue the strips around the edges of the spiral, creating smooth railings so the marbles won't drop off the path (Figure ⑫).

3. Trace and cut out four copies of the Small Braces, and glue one to each side of both Large Braces with their holes in alignment (Figure ⑬).

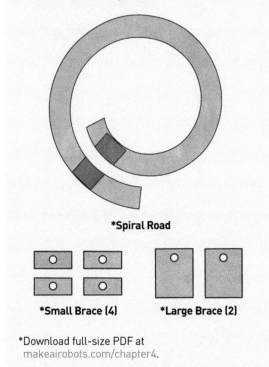

YOU WILL NEED:
- Stencils*
- Cardboard
- Hot glue
- Pencil or chopstick

*Spiral Road

*Small Brace (4)   *Large Brace (2)

*Download full-size PDF at makeairobots.com/chapter4.

4. Using the shaded areas on the Spiral Road stencil as a guide, glue these completed braces onto the bottom of your track. The two pieces should face each other, and the holes should almost overlap (Figures ⑭ and ⑮).

5. Thread a pencil or chopstick through these holes, and vertically spread the tracks apart Figure ⑯). (You might need a bit of glue to hold them in place.)

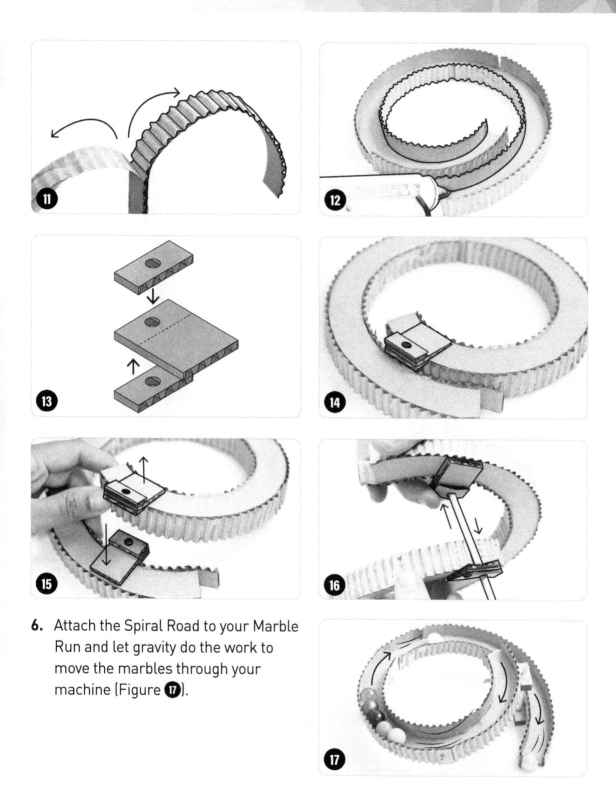

6. Attach the Spiral Road to your Marble Run and let gravity do the work to move the marbles through your machine (Figure **17**).

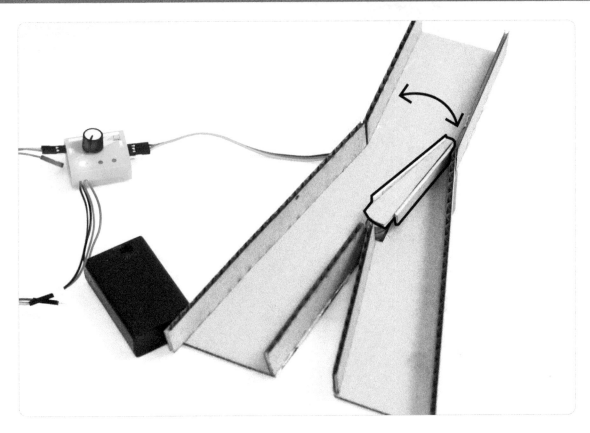

The servo motors we talked about in the Introduction can be a real game changer for your inventions: They're small and easy to attach to materials and can even hook up to a micro:bit with a little coding. (We will get to that soon!)

Servos are different from the DC motors we used in our car projects; they have internal gears, a position sensor, and a control circuit. Although they are slower,

servos are precise with their movements and are adjustable with a servo tester, a small device that can control the servo.

An interesting way to add variety to your Marble Run is to have multiple paths for the marbles to travel. By simply adding a servo and a bit of cardboard to the end of a pathway, we create a way to randomly divert your marbles to different routes.

YOU WILL NEED:

- Hot glue
- Stencils*
- Servo motor
- Servo tester
- Three-battery holder (for 4.5 V)
- Batteries
- Wires
- Popsicle sticks (optional)

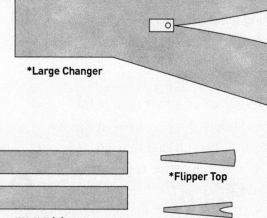

*Large Changer

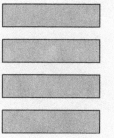

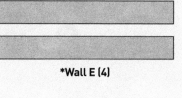

*Flipper Top

*Wall E (4)

*Flipper Middle

*Flipper Bottom

*Wall C (4)

*Download the full-size PDF at makeairobots.com/chapter4.

SERVO LANE CHANGER

1. Start by tracing and cutting out the pieces from the Stencil Library. Using some hot glue — and an adult's help, if necessary — glue two of the Wall C pieces on the outer sides of the Lane Changer (Figure ⓲).

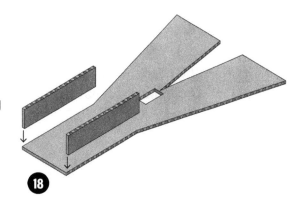

18

2. Glue the other two Wall C pieces into a V shape alongside the inner split of the Lane Changer (Figure **19**).

3. Glue the two Wall E pieces onto the remaining sides so there are rails splitting a single path into two paths (Figure **20**).

4. Glue the Flipper Top and Flipper Bottom pieces to either side of the Flipper Middle. Make sure that the points are lined up together so they're all sandwiched together (Figure **21**).

    When stacked, the three pieces of the Flipper will leave a small notch exposed.

5. For cleaner sides, glue Popsicle sticks to the sides of the Flipper, to hide the three stacked layers of cardboard with the Popsicle sticks' smooth surface (Figure **22**).

6. Once the glue has dried, you'll need the small **servo horn**, a small arm

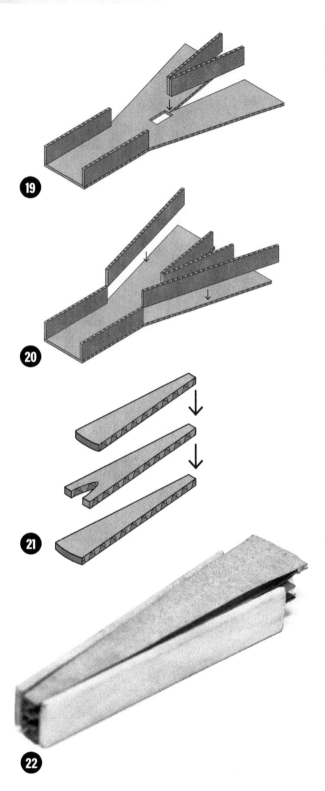

19

20

21

22

attached to the servo motor and used to make another object move. (Figure **23**).

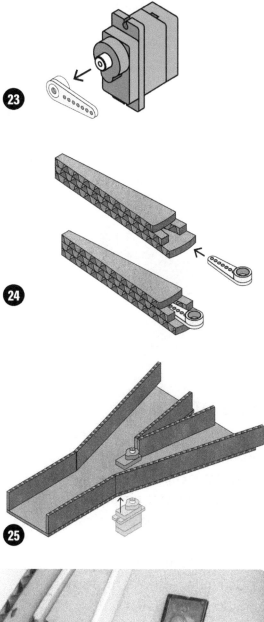

7. Cover the arm of the servo horn with a little bit of hot glue and push it into the middle of the Flipper's notch. We'll attach it to the servo later (Figure **24**).

8. Flip your Lane Changer over and slide the servo into the hole from the bottom. Keep the small white circle on top of the motor close to the top of the Y (Figure **25**).

9. Adjust the servo's position so only the blue circle and the white gear are sticking up and the rest of the servo is nearly flat with the cardboard (Figure **26**).

Attach the Flipper to the servo with the servo horn's hole, and you're ready to roll. Hook the servo up to the servo tester and the three-battery holder, and set the tester to Automatic. Your Flipper will swing back and forth like a window wiper, ready to divert your marbles toward a random path.

Where will each path lead? Will one path be longer, and the other be a shortcut? Will one go straight toward the finish line, while the other goes down the fancy Spiral Road? Or perhaps one goes to a dead end? The possibilities are endless!

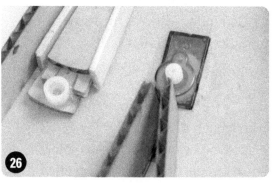

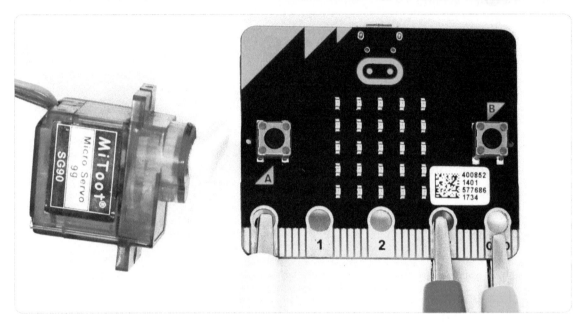

MICRO:BIT

YOU WILL NEED:

- Completed Lane Changer
- Servo motor
- Alligator clips (optionally with a male connector pin at the end)
- Wire cutters and electrical tape (optional)
- Micro:bit and USB
- Computer with internet access
- Button (optional)

Find starter and finished micro:bit code for guidance at: makeairobots.com/chapter4

Even though a servo tester is a fun way to set the movement of servo motors (see page 96), the micro:bit can offer us a chance to program a series of movements and activate them with the push of a button.

This project uses the micro:bit's buttons to control the Flipper's ability to send marbles down one path of the Lane Changer or the other. We're going to code a way to precisely position the Flipper, and then we'll activate the code.

Before jumping into the coding, we need to cover the process of connecting a servo to your micro:bit. This may seem a bit tricky at first, but by the time you finish this book, you'll be such an expert that you'll be able to teach your friends.

CODE LIBRARY

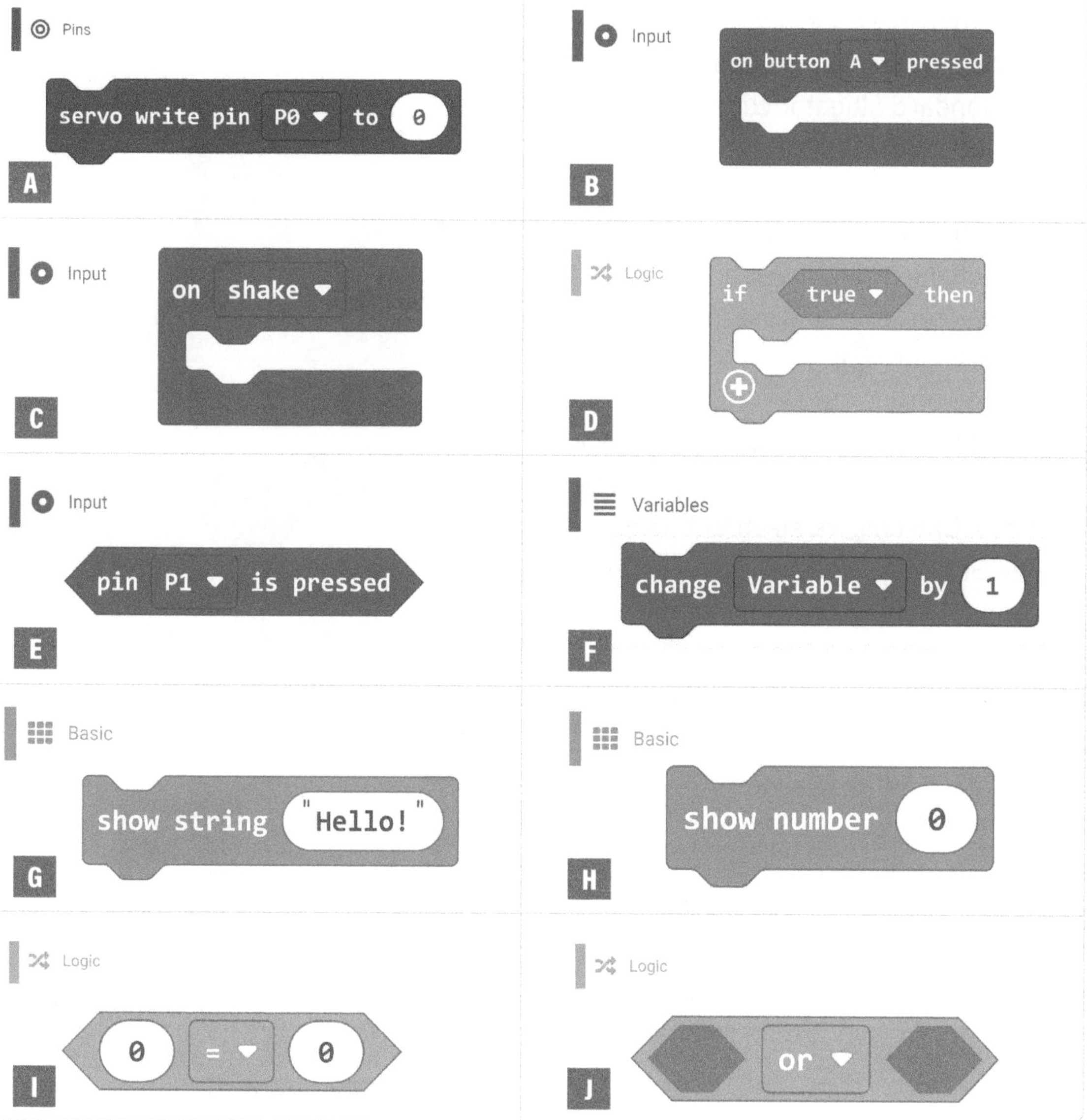

◎ Pins

servo write pin P0 ▼ to 0

A

● Input

on button A ▼ pressed

B

● Input

on shake ▼

C

⚄ Logic

if true ▼ then
⊕

D

● Input

pin P1 ▼ is pressed

E

≡ Variables

change Variable ▼ by 1

F

▦ Basic

show string "Hello!"

G

▦ Basic

show number 0

H

⚄ Logic

0 = ▼ 0

I

⚄ Logic

or ▼

J

We strongly recommend using alligator clips that have a pin at the end (Figure 27), readily available online or at electronics stores. This pin plugs into the connectors at the end of the servo. If you have this type of connector, skip to step 3; otherwise, step 1 and 2 show how to adjust standard alligator clips for this project.

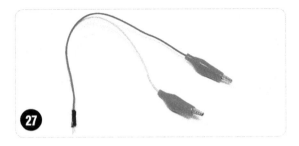

1. With an adult's help, use wire cutters to strip off the plastic insulation of the servo wires, exposing the metal wiring inside (Figure 28).

2. Connect an alligator clip to each of the exposed wires. There should be three wires: One positive electrical wire, one GND wire, and one signal wire for communicating with the micro:bit.

    Separate the wires a bit so the alligator clips don't touch — this will cause the servo to stop working (Figure 29).

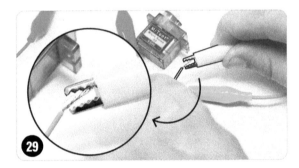

3. Each wire needs to connect to a specific pin on your micro:bit. See the "Connecting Your Servo" sidebar on the right for connection instructions (Figure 30).

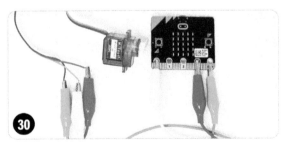

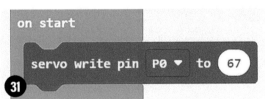

With your servo connected to the micro:bit, it's time to write the code that will tell it what to do. Head on over to makecode.microbit.org and start up a new project called Servo Gate.

For this project, we want the servo to move to one side when we press the A button and move to the opposite side when we press B, giving us control over the marble's path. We already know how to enable the micro:bit's buttons to control actions (see page 42), so we just need to learn how to use the servo blocks.

1. Click the Advanced drawer toward the bottom and then click on the Pins drawer, and near the bottom you will see the Servo Write Pin [P0] to **A** block. Drag it into the On Start code mouth and set the pin to the pin connected to your servo (pin 0) (Figure **31**).

The number bubble at the end sets the angle to which our servo will turn. This might take a few tries to figure out the best number for your Marble Run. Our tests show 67 and 117 were good angles for the Flipper to cleanly divert the marbles toward their intended path, but you should test different numbers to determine the best angles for your build. Choosing one of the numbers will set your flipper to one side when the power is connected.

2. After you add a servo to your MakeCode project, you'll see the micro:bit, the servo, and its connections in the testing window (Figure **32**).

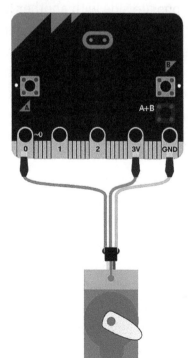

32

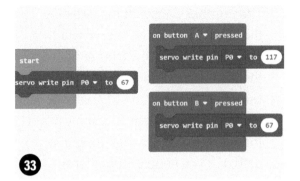

33

34

This animation not only helps us remember the wiring but also lets us test the servo in the window without having to redownload the code every time a change is made.

3. Use two On Button [ ] Pressed **B** code mouths to activate our buttons: Set the A button to move the servo to the opposite side with another Servo Write Pin [P0] to **A** block, and then set the other On Button [ ] Pressed **B** code mouth to **B**, and use the Servo Write Pin [P0] to **A** block to return the Flipper back to where it started (Figure **33**).

Now you can download your code to the micro:bit (see page 13), and your Flipper should now block a lane if the A button is pressed and move over to block the other lane if the B button is pressed. You may need to test and adjust the angle numbers you've assigned to the servo to make sure a lane is completely blocked and there isn't any opening for a marble to sneak

by — no matter how well you test in the website's preview window, there's always fine-tuning that needs to happen in the real world!

TAKING IT FURTHER

The micro:bit's buttons are cool, but they're rather tiny. Sometimes it's nice to just have a big button to push so you don't have to be so dainty. There are many, many different kinds of buttons, ranging from teeny tiny to as big as your hand; we're going to use our personal favorite, called an arcade switch (Figure **34**).

Believe it or not, you already learned how to hook this button up in chapter 3 — it's as simple as coding any other device we attach to a pin!

And we're going to use a neat coding trick where the servo will move to one side when the button is held down and then spring back to the other side when you release it, all with just a few lines of code.

1. Start by using alligator clips to connect your button to the micro:bit. The button's negative prong should go to the micro:bit's GND pin (Figure **35**).

   It's OK for the servo's negative wire and the button's negative wire to both be connected to the GND pin, and one can be clipped to the other if they don't fit.

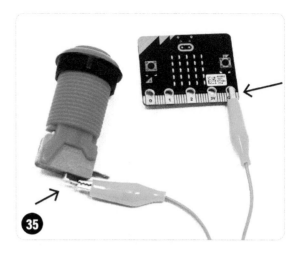

35

2. Attach the button's positive prong to an available pin that will not be used by the servo (Figure **36**).

3. Jump back to makecode.microbit.org.

   In the Forever block, place an If [True] Then **D** statement from the Logic drawer.

   If you look in the Input drawer, there is a special hexagon-shaped block named Pin [ ] Is Pressed **E** that can be placed over the [True] option in your If [true] Then **D** statement.

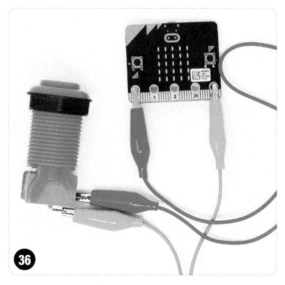

36

4. Make sure the pin is set to whichever pin you connected your button's positive wire.

   Place a Servo Write Pin [P0] to **A** block in the mouth of your If statement, and set the angle so the Flipper will move to one side (Figure **37**).

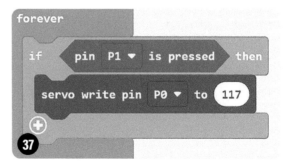

37

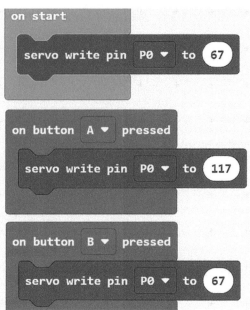

The If statement should tell the micro:bit, "If the button is pressed, move the servo here."

5. Click the little + button at the bottom of the If statement to add another condition; it should now also have an **else** mouth — this means anything that *does not* make the If statement true will activate the "else" code instead.

Place a servo block in the "else" mouth to move the flipper back to the opposite position you set. Now your micro:bit knows what to do if the button is not held down (Figure **38**).

Download the code into your micro:bit, and you now have a working button that will divert marbles toward a specific path — until you let go of the button!

SETTING UP THE AI CODE

You've had a bit of practice with your AI projects through the first three chapters, and have been successfully using our starter code to enable your micro:bit to understand the data sent from the Micro:bit of AI website. But downloading and using our pre-assembled starter code is a shortcut. Now that you have a better understanding of MakeCode, you're going to learn how to build your own starter code from scratch!

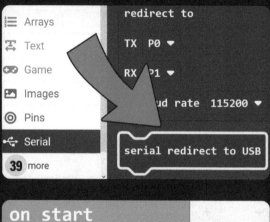

1. The first thing you need to do is open a channel for the micro:bit to reach the AI. You'll do this by using the Serial Redirect to USB block in the Serial drawer, which will appear if you click on the Advanced drawer. The Serial drawer contains blocks that enable you to control data being sent to and from the micro:bit (Figure 39).

2. Drag the Serial Redirect to USB block into the On Start block, and it should snap into place. This will tell the micro:bit to listen for information being sent from your computer through a USB cable to your micro:bit every time you turn on the micro:bit. This is how the Micro:bit of AI website and your micro:bit will "talk" (Figure 40).

3. Open the Serial drawer again, find the Serial on Data Received (New Line ( )) block, and drag it onto your workspace (Figure 41).

The Serial on Data Received (New Line ( )) block tells the micro:bit what to do when information is being sent. It's listening for a special "New Line ( )" signal that the Micro:bit of AI website adds to every class name being sent to your micro:bit. When the block detects that signal, it will activate the rest of the code we're about to add.

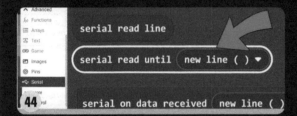

4. As we covered in Chapter 3, we can use a variable to save the information that gets sent, so it can be used later. Open the Variable drawer and click the Make a Variable button. We've named this variable "SerialData" because that's exactly what it is—data that will be sent over the serial line (Figure **42**).

5. Once you've created the SerialData variable, some new blocks will appear in the Variables drawer—including the Set (SerialData) to (0) block.

Drag a Set (SerialData) to (0) block into the Serial On Data Received (New Line ( )) block you just placed on your workspace (Figure **43**).

6. Now we just need to tell this variable what information to save.

Back in the Serial drawer, find the Serial Read Until New Line ( ) bubble. Drag this bubble and place it over the "0" in the Set (SerialData) to (0) block you just added—it should snap into place and replace the "0" (Figure **39**).

Now when a class name is sent from the **Make: AI Robots** website, this block of code will take that information and store it inside the SerialData variable.

7. The final thing you need is a bit of code that tells the micro:bit what to do when it receives a specific class name. To do this, you need to add some If statements.

Open the Logic drawer and grab an If (True) Then block, and place it just below your variable code in the Forever block (Figure **45**).

8. Back in the Logic drawer, find the " "
    (=) " " hexagon and place it over the
    word "True" in the If statement—it
    should replace the "True" hexagon
    (Figure **46**).

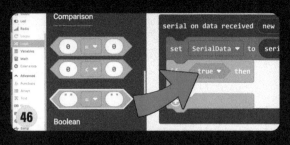

9. Back in the Variable drawer, drag a
    SerialData bubble over to replace the
    first " " of the " " (=) " " bubble. As you
    drag it near the first spot, a little red
    dot and line will appear to indicate
    where it's aligned (Figure **47**).

10. The second " " is what you've already
    been editing in each project, the name
    of one of the classes you've trained.

    Once you replace the blank " " variable
    with a variable for one of your trained
    classes, it will compare SerialData with
    the class name you created. If the two
    text strings match, it will activate any
    code in the If statement (**Figure 48**).

    In our example, if the SerialData
    matches "Class Name", the micro:bit
    will activate its LEDs in the shape of
    a heart.

    Click the little + at the bottom of the
    If Statement to add more If statement
    options, and repeat the code for
    each class that you've trained for
    your project.

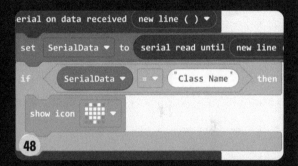

And that's it!

You've now created your own starter code
from scratch, and should use the rest of
the projects in this book to practice so
you no longer need to rely on our pre-
assembled starter code. It may take more
time to create the code from scratch, but
it'll make you a better coder and give you
more control over your robots.

You may need to keep referring back
to this section at first, but with a little
practice you'll intuitively know what to do!

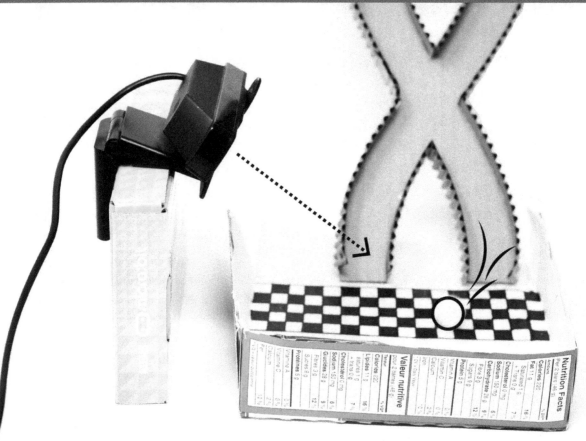

YOU WILL NEED:

- Marble Run and finish line
- Alligator clips
- Micro:bit and USB
- Webcam
- Computer with internet access
- Marbles (of different colors)

For links to the AI tools, explore resources at:
makeairobots.com/chapter4

By now, I bet your workspace has become one giant Marble Run. Have you tried to race the marbles yet and see which can complete your gauntlet first?

They can go so fast and sometimes it can be challenging to determine exactly which one crosses the finish line first. This seems like a job for the precision of a computer — or our AI helper.

In this project, we're going to teach the AI

to recognize all of your marbles and then use that data to decide which one it saw cross the finish line first.

THE TRAINING

Build a finish line to celebrate your winning marble. This will be where the AI looks for the winner, recognizing a change has occurred when a marble crosses over it. Set up a webcam at this end so your AI can record the data it needs.

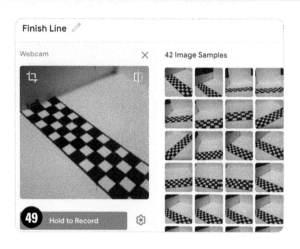

1. On the Teachable Machine website (teachablemachine.withgoogle.com), create a new Image Project and take a bunch of photos of the empty finish line from different angles and positions. Make sure you can see as much of it as possible in the photos. This will serve as the "before" reference images that will change after a marble crosses the finish line (Figure **49**).

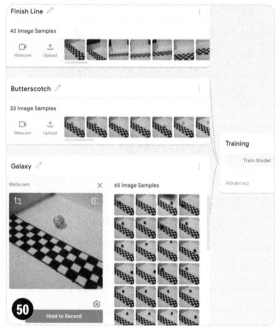

2. Add classes for all the marble competitors. We're just going to show a race between only two marbles in this example — named Butterscotch and Galaxy — but you can create classes for each marble you're using (Figure **50**).

3. When you've taken at least 20 photos of each marble at the finishing line in different spots, train and test your AI in the preview window to see how well it can identify them.

Notice how the AI can't give a proper answer when there is more than one marble in the area? That's OK, because the Make: AI Robots website has a way to get around that problem. Just make sure the AI has enough reference pictures to clearly tell when one marble crosses the line (Figure **51**).

When you're happy with the results, the last step is to save them. Click on the Export Model button in the Preview column, which will bring up a new window; select Upload My Model to save your AI model to your browser. Copy the shareable URL link so you can use it as a database after you've created the micro:bit code.

THE CODING

Although the AI and the Make: AI Robots website are going to do all the work in identifying which marble won, it's your job to decide what to do with that information. In this project, we're going to have the micro:bit keep score of our races and determine the winner of a "best two out of three" competition.

To do this, we're going to take the quarter-tracking code from chapter 3's coin detector (see page 76) and modify it to track our marble winners.

51

1. Open a new browser window and go to makecode.microbit.org to begin this new microbit project. Start with the starter code we use to connect to our AI website (see page 107), as well as the code that we used to identify quarters from chapter 3 (see page 79).

Add new variables to represent each individual marble class, as well as their scores. In our case, we've created variables named Butterscotch and Galaxy, and ButterscotchScore and GalaxyScore (Figure **52**).

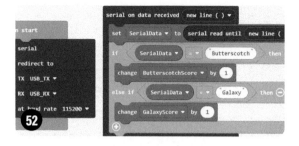

From the Variables drawer, drag a Change [Variable] by (1) **F** block into each class's If statement. Choose the correct variable to match the different marble-name classes.

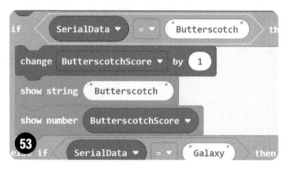

2. From the Basic drawer, add the Show String **G** block and change the text string to a marble's class name.

   Also from the Basic drawer, add the Show Number **H** block below the Show String **G** block. From the Variables drawer, drag the matching marble-score variable you created into the Show Number **H** block.

   In our example, the code should tell the AI that if the SerialData shows that Butterscotch is the first marble at the finish line, then ButterscotchScore should increase by one point. Then, the text string Butterscotch should be displayed, followed by the number for ButterscotchScore (Figure **53**).

Do the same for your other marble classes, so the winning marble's name and score will be able to be displayed no matter which wins.

Remember, if you have more than two marble classes, simply click the + symbol on the If statement to create another possible outcome.

3. In order to determine if there has been a winner, the code needs to check all the variables to see if one has hit your race-winning score. There are usually a few ways to solve any coding problem; for our projects, we try to be efficient and use the one that takes the least amount of lines.

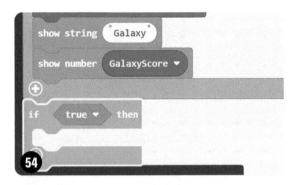

Instead of adding an extra If statement to each class section to see if each marble's score has reached the score goal, add a single If statement **D** below the existing one — we're going to make it check all the variables at the same time (Figure **54**).

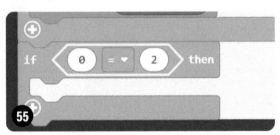

4. From the Logic drawer, drag a (0) = (0) **I** comparison hexagon onto the new If statement'sTrue bubble, replacing it. Leave the first zero alone for the moment, but change the second zero to whatever you want the winning score to be; in our example, we chose 2 (Figure **55**).

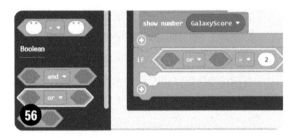

5. Go back to the Logic drawer and drag the 0 or 0 **J** into the first zero of the If statement to replace it (Figure **56**).

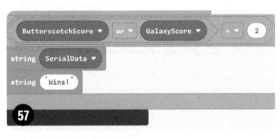

6. Open the Variable drawer and place each marble scoring variable in an empty slot of your If statement. In our example, this code now checks whether ButterscotchScore or GalaxyScore equals 2, and if either does, it will perform an action (Figure **57**).

All that's left to do is to add an action code that will be activated when a winner is detected. We used a Show String **G** block and dragged the little

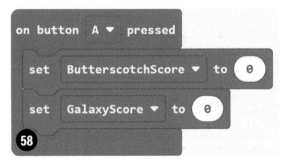

SerialData bubble from the Variable Menu and placed it the (text field) block to display the winning marble's name and declare it the winner.

But you can use the coding skills you've learned in the previous chapters to create your own winning indicator: Instead of a text message, what about an LED picture on the screen? Or how about a victory song?

7. Last, add code to reset all of your variables back to zero so you can play

again. In this case, we're using the A button to reset our scores back to zero (Figure **58**).

BRINGING IT TO LIFE

To get your Marble Race ready for the green light, head over to the Make: AI Robots website, pair your micro:bit, and paste in the Teachable Machine link you copied from the Training section. You can even reuse the scoreboard idea from chapter 3 to make it look fancy.

There's actually a small problem with the way the AI website judges these races. Run through a race and see if you can find out what we mean. Did you catch it (Figure 59)?

Run your race again and watch the AI screen and the message log. The AI can clearly pick up the first marble to cross the line, but once more marbles start to pile in, the AI gets a little confused since we never trained it to notice more than one marble in the finishing area. The AI may even select the second- or third-place finisher as the winner immediately after selecting the first (Figure 60).

This clearly won't do. To fix this, we need to click on the gear icon in the top right of the screen. This adds a little toggle next to each class where we can switch it from "always-watching" mode to "one-winner" mode. This tells the AI to stop after it detects one class and to wait for you to reset it. Turn this setting on for each of your marble racers, and the first marble past the finish line will be identified as the

winner even as more marbles cross (Figure 61).

If you watch the message log, you will see that only one of the stop-and-hold categories is being sent now and should be activating whatever you've coded onto your micro:bit.

And with that, you're all set! Race your marbles from as far away as you'd like with the confidence that the computer will be able to tell you who won!

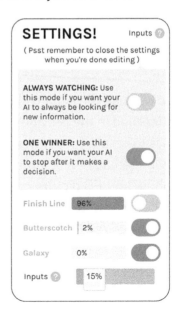

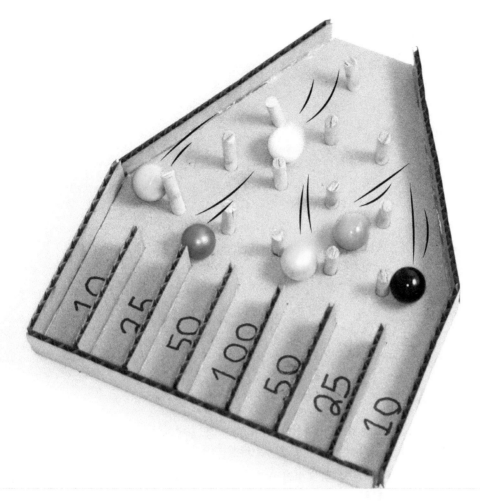

TAKING IT FURTHER

Need more ideas to get your creativity racing? Try out some of these extra project ideas to make your Marble Run more elaborate.

We designed a starting gate, but what about a way to end your Marble Run? Using the Wall stencils, try designing something like the design shown above, using small wooden pegs that will cause your marbles to ricochet all over the place, ending in pockets with bonus point values. You can still train your AI to identify which marble comes in first place, but the bonuses can determine which marble is the luckiest!

Or you could think about different obstacles — the design of a fidget spinner works perfectly to throw some chaos into your Marble Run. These can be built with an axle from chapter 2, using a straw

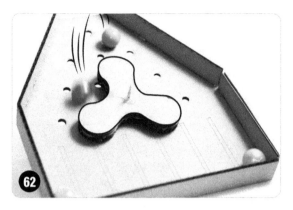

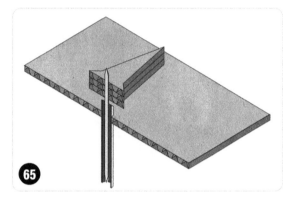

mounted underneath as a shaft and a thin wooden stick glued through the middle of the spinner that acts as the axle spinning inside the straw (Figures **62** through **65**).

If you have metal ball bearings that can be used instead of marbles, you can create a series of open circuits like you used in chapter 3's Ball Toss game to add some fancy lighting effects. As the metal ball bearing rolls across the copper tape, it will complete the circuit and momentarily activate the light (Figure **66**).

Use the Wall stencils and design a rail system in your track for the metal ball

bearings to follow. If you position the walls slightly narrower than the metal ball bearings, the ball will slide down the rail system's channel, momentarily completing each circuit to create a series of blinking lights as the ball rolls by (Figure **67**).

And don't forget how we wanted to automate our starting gate! Swap out the straw hinge for a servo motor, gluing the gate to the servo horn (Figure **68**). (It may be easiest to detach the horn before gluing, and then reattaching the whole horn/gate piece to the servo after the glue dries.

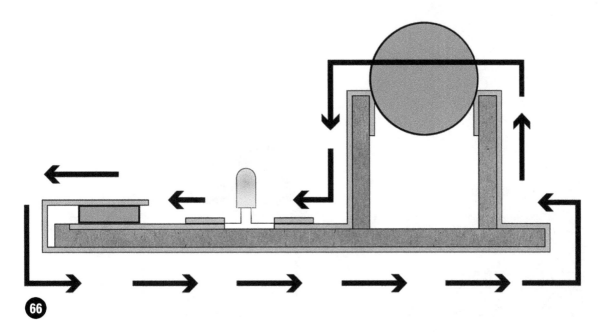

66

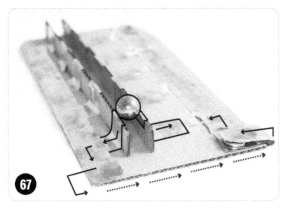

67

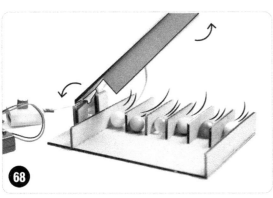

68

WRAPPING UP

Unfortunately, it's time to wrap up our lessons on Marble Runs. But that doesn't mean you have to stop building! Remember, these are just an inspiration for you to use in creating your own Marble Runs.

And don't stress if you had a hard time with any of these sections. We've started getting into more complicated builds that are going to challenge you in new ways. Even your failed projects can still end up as successful obstacles somewhere along your track. No one has ever built a Marble Run and said they wanted *less* parts!

5

LINKAGES

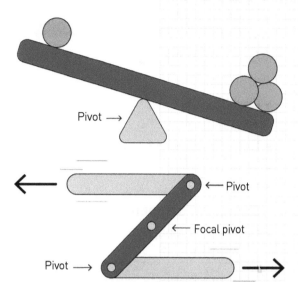

Pivot →

← Pivot

← Focal pivot

Pivot →

Adobe Stock-Mykola

Have you ever wondered how a seesaw works? Or how objects as small as lamps or as large as construction vehicles have more than one main moving part? These are examples of a simple machine called a **lever**.

A lever is a mechanism that uses a pivot to help add strength to move an object. Besides helping us lift and move things, we can turn levers from a simple machine into a complex machine by adding two or more levers together to create a **linkage**. Linkages change the direction of motion with normal pivots that enable parts to rotate, as well as focal pivots to provide structure.

We're going to use linkages to create a Leopard with moving legs, as well as automate those legs with a servo. Then we'll use a micro:bit to control those movements so it can run — and walk — at the touch of a button. Finally, we'll create an AI to control the Leopard by mimicking our own movements.

CHALLENGE CHECKLIST:

- **Build a Leopard with linkage legs**
- **Add a servo to automate its leg movements**
- **Use a micro:bit as a controller**
- **Create AI to direct our Leopard through body language**

YOU WILL NEED:

- Stencils*
- Cardboard
- Hole punch
- Hot-glue gun and glue sticks
- Tape
- Straws
- Scissors and a hobby knife
- Construction paper

* Two 15-hole Linkage Bars with holes in 5 and 8
(Linkage Bar A)

* Two 8-hole Linkage Bars with holes in 1 and 2
(Linkage Bar B)

* One 8-hole Linkage Bar with holes in 1 and 8
(Linkage Bar C)

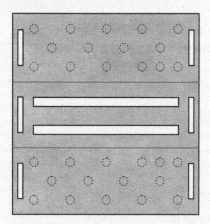

* Body

*Download full-size PDF at
makeairobots.com/chapter5.

When you locate the Linkage Bar in the Stencil Library, you may scratch your head over its design. This stencil has multiple holes marked so you can use it to make linkage bars of different lengths and with different hole placements — just trace it to the size you need and mark where the necessary holes should go. When we ask you to punch holes in a Linkage Bar, we will note their locations by counting from hole 1 at the left.

But don't punch out every hole; the more holes you punch, the weaker the Linkage Bar becomes.

A standard hole punch should cut through the cardboard, although you may need an adult's help because of its thickness. And if the holes aren't large enough, poke a pencil through the hole and wiggle the pencil around to stretch out the hole.

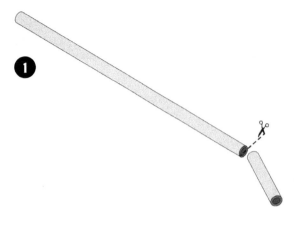

MECHANICAL LEOPARD

1. Trace onto paper, glue onto cardboard, and cut the following: two 15-hole Linkage Bars with holes in 5 and 8 (Linkage Bar A), two 8-hole Linkage Bars with holes in 1 and 2 (Linkage Bar B), and one 8-hole Linkage Bar with holes in 1 and 8 (Linkage Bar C).

   Measure and cut pieces of straw into four 1½-inch pieces. These will be our pivot pins, which will hold the linkages together and enable them to rotate (Figure ❶).

2. Tightly wrap tape around one end of each piece. As with the hinges in chapter 1, the tape will prevent these pivot pins from sliding out of their holes (Figure ❷).

3. Place a pivot pin through hole 5 of a Linkage Bar A, making sure the tape is layered thick enough to prevent it from slipping all the way through (Figure ❸).

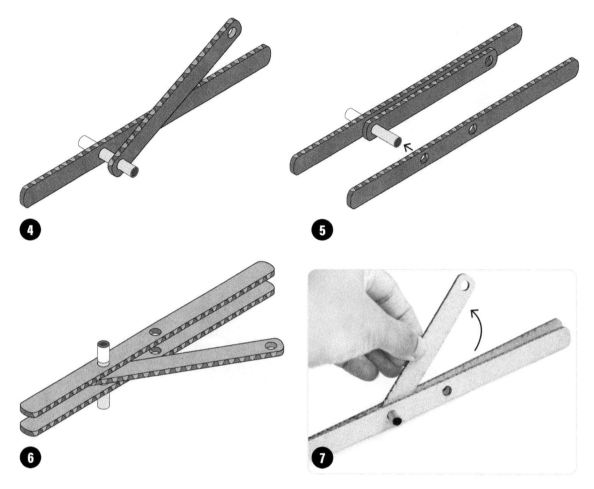

4. Attach a Linkage Bar C to the pivot pin in Linkage Bar A, using Linkage Bar C's hole 1 (Figure **4**).

5. Attach the second Linkage Bar A to the pivot point, using that piece's hole 5 so Linkage Bar C is sandwiched between the two Linkage Bar A pieces (Figures **5** through **7**).

Secure the linkages on the pivot pin by wrapping tape around the other end, leaving just enough room for the linkages to rotate on the pivot pin.

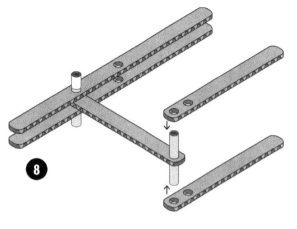

8

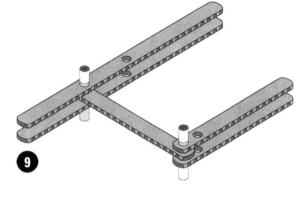

9

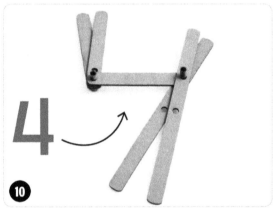

10

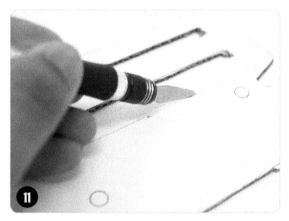

11

6. Use a pivot pin to attach one of the two Linkage Bar B pieces on each side of Linkage Bar C, using hole 1 of Linkage Bar B. The structure should resemble the numeral 4 (Figures **8**, **9**, and **10**).

Tape the other end of the pivot pin to secure everything in place.

7. Trace, glue onto cardboard, and cut the entire Body Section from the Stencil Library.

Ask an adult for help on this part, because it's delicate: Lightly score the red lines of the Body Section. (*Scoring* means to cut just the top layer of the cardboard, not all the way through to the other side, to enable the cardboard to easily bend.)

Cut the long slots out of the body — this is where the top of the levers will poke through to control the linkages (Figure **11**).

8. Bend the sides away from the cut to a 90-degree angle and add hot glue to the edge to help them maintain a squared frame (Figure **12**).

9. Measure and cut two 3-inch pivot pins from a straw.

Line up hole 2 in the shorter Linkage Bar B with the holes on the side of the Body Section. Insert a 3-inch pivot pin through one side of the Body Section, through hole 2 of Linkage Bar B, and through the other side of the Body Section. Add tape to the ends to secure it in place (Figures **13** and **14**).

12

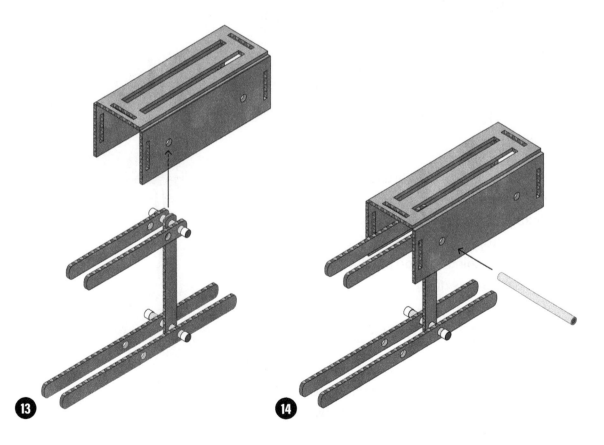

13

14

10. Line up hole 8 on the longer Linkage Bar A and secure it with the other 3-inch pivot pin, with the long end of the bar sticking through the slots at the top of the Body Section. Add tape to the ends to keep it in place (Figure **15**).

With the long end of Linkage Bar A sticking through the slots at the top of the Body Section, line up hole 8 in the longer Linkage Bar A with the holes on the side of the Body Section (Figure **16**).

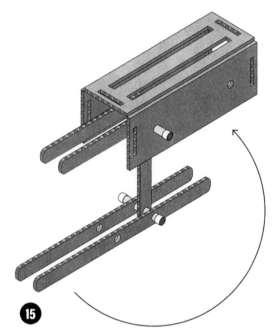

15

Insert the other 3-inch pivot pin through one side of the Body Section, through hole 8 of Linkage Bar A, and through the other side of the Body Section. Add tape to the ends of the pivot pin to secure it in place (Figure **17**).

The skeleton of your Leopard is now complete! With the focal pivots securing the linkage structure, you can move the lever at the top and see how the legs move in a bounding fashion just like a real leopard's legs do.

16

TAKING IT FURTHER

Use construction paper, pens, and other craft supplies to add a head and decorate your Leopard to give it some personality. And don't forget a name!

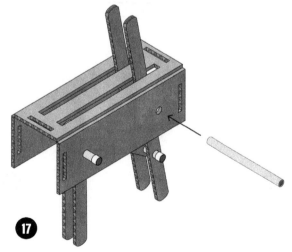

17

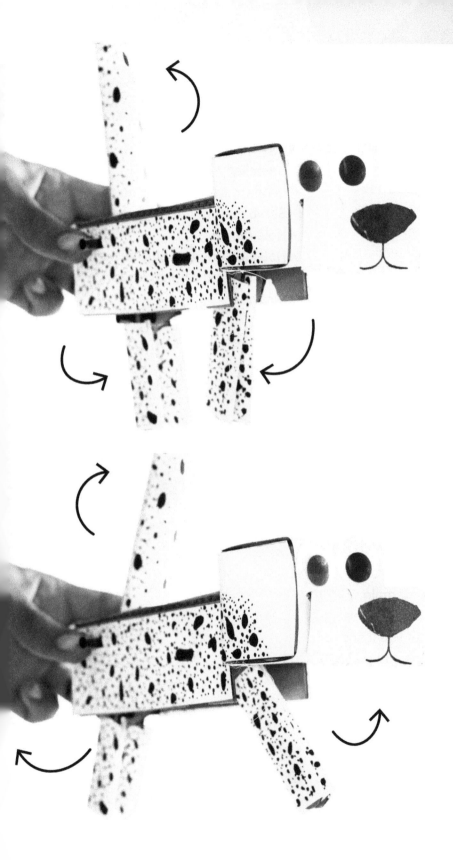

There are plenty of ways you can get creative with the electronics you've learned so far: You can add LEDs as light-up eyes, or a buzzer to make your Leopard growl. But our next project builds off the linkages we built, adding a servo motor to power its legs.

SERVO-POWERED LEGS

If you were looking for the super-quick solution, you *could* cut away some of the body and glue the servo to one of the legs and call your project done — that *would* work. But we're going to add a second linkage to the existing system to demonstrate how complex linkage systems aren't actually that complex.

1. Placing the servo will be the first important task. For this example, we're going to choose an area close to the Leopard's head, but you'll see later that linkages allow you to place this servo pretty much anywhere.

   Mount your servo so the servo horn can rotate toward the tail (Figure **18**).

YOU WILL NEED:

- Stencils*
- Leopard from the previous project
- Servo motor with single horn
- Hole punch
- Hot-glue gun and glue sticks
- Scissors and a hobby knife
- Straws
- Tape
- Servo tester
- Batteries and wires

*3-Hole Linkage Bar

*6-Hole Linkage Bar

*Download full-size PDF at makeairobots.com/chapter5.

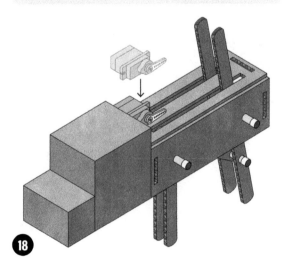

18

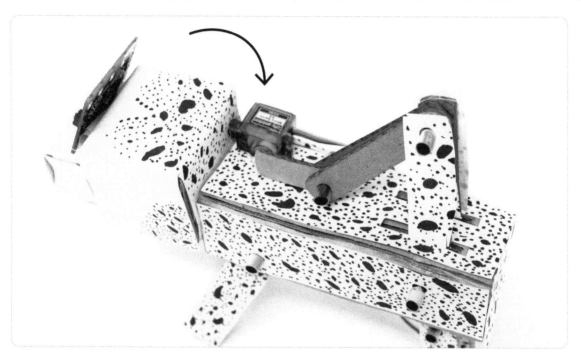

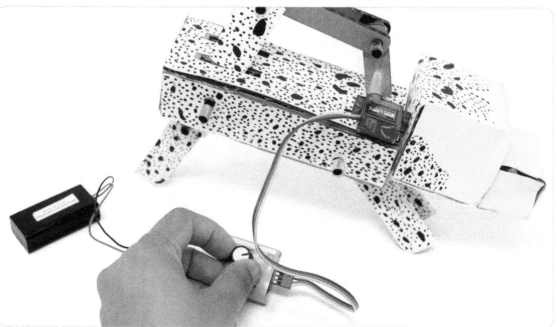

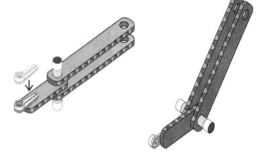

19

2. Trace onto paper, glue onto cardboard, and cut the following: two 3-hole Linkage Bars with a hole in 1 (Linkage Bar D) and two 6-hole Linkage Bars with holes in 1 and 6 (Linkage Bar E).

Sandwich Linkage Bar D between the two Linkage Bar E pieces and align the holes. Cut and insert a pivot pin through the holes, securing the ends with tape.

Glue the other end of Linkage Bar D to the servo horn (Figure **19**).

3. Connect the servo horn (and the new linkage system) to the servo motor.

With the servo horn pointing as far toward the head (or straight up, depending how you set up your servo motor's position and range of motion), push the existing tail lever also toward the head (so the back legs stretch backward). Extend the

Linkage Bar D pieces toward the tail lever and mark the tail lever where they overlap.

Cut a hole in the tail lever and use a pivot pin to attach the free end of the Linkage Bar D pieces to the tail lever. Secure the pivot pin with tape on its ends.

You may need to adjust where Linkage Bar D and the tail lever are

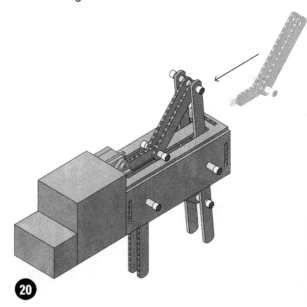

20

connected, depending on the angles and position of your servo. The higher up the tail that you connect Linkage Bar D, the less the servo has to move to move the legs (Figures **20** and **21**).

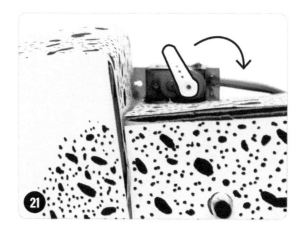

4. Attach the servo to the servo tester and the servo tester to the battery. Turn on the servo to bring your Leopard to life (Figures **22** and **23**)!

TAKING IT FURTHER

Now that you have working models of linkages, you can see how the servo can actually be mounted just about anywhere — as long as you build a linkage system that can connect it to the main tail lever. You can even mount the servo on the Leopard's rear to help hide the wires. Changing and experimenting with the length and number of linkages creates new possibilities with this project and others.

Notes:

MICRO:BIT

YOU WILL NEED:

- Micro:bit & USB cable
- Computer with internet access
- Leopard with servo motor
- Alligator clip–to–male pin connector cables

Find starter and finished micro:bit code for guidance at: makeairobots.com/chapter5

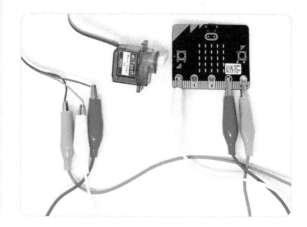

CODE LIBRARY

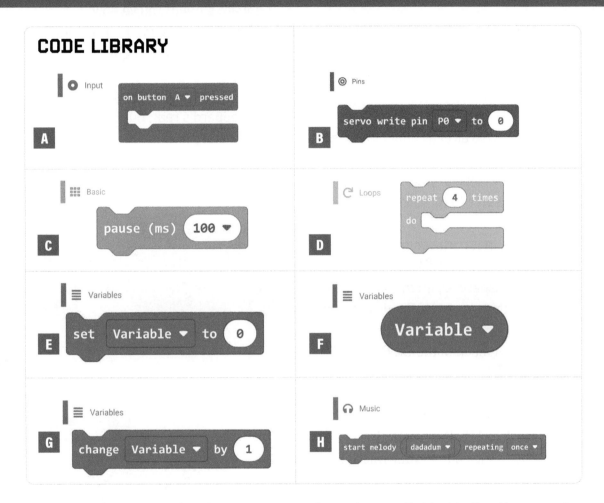

A Input

on button A ▼ pressed

B Pins

servo write pin P0 ▼ to 0

C Basic

pause (ms) 100 ▼

D Loops

repeat 4 times
do

E Variables

set Variable ▼ to 0

F Variables

Variable ▼

G Variables

change Variable ▼ by 1

H Music

start melody dadadum ▼ repeating once ▼

Our Leopard can move, but the next step is having it move on *command*.

We'll use the micro:bit as our controller, but that requires us to connect it to our servo motor. You already have experience in connecting a servo to the micro:bit, but look back at the Lane Changer project from chapter 4's Marble Run if you need a refresher (see page 100).

The Lane Changer moved at only one speed to divert marbles, but animals like our Leopard should be able to move at different speeds. This project will show how we can program the micro:bit to control the speed of the servo, enabling our Leopard to run *and* walk.

As with all our coding projects, go to makecode.microbit.org to build our code, and create a new project called Living Leopard.

1. With the servo already attached to the tail lever, we want to create code to tell the micro:bit at what positions we want the servo to move in each stride.

From the Input drawer, move two On Button (A) Pressed **A** blocks onto your workspace. Open the Advanced drawer, then open the Pin drawer, and place a Servo Write Pin (P0) to (180) **B** block in each of the On Button (A) Pressed **A** blocks.

2. Set the servo command for one Button A to 125 degrees and download the code to your micro:bit (see page 13). Disconnect the servo horn from the motor and then press Button A; this should spin the little white gear all the way to its end

position. Reattach the servo horn so it points toward the top of the Leopard's head: You've now calibrated your servo to a starting point (Figures 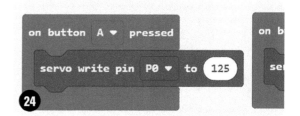 24 and 25).

3. We need the servo to swing toward the Leopard's rear, but that number is a mystery at this time — we know only that it needs to be less than 125 degrees.

26

Set the other On Button (A) Pressed
[A] block to button B, and set its Servo
Write Pin to different degrees until you
find the angle that positions your
Leopard to stand straight up — on our
project, 45 worked best, but your
angles may be different (Figure **26**).

After a bit of trial and error, you
should be able to make your Leopard
run by repeatedly pressing the
buttons A and B.

4. Now that you've figured out the angles
to manually make your Leopard run,
we're going to add code to run several
steps with a single button press.

Open the Pin drawer (remember, it's
part of the Advanced drawer), and add
another Servo Write Pin (P0) to (180)
[B] block under the Servo Write Pin
(P0) to (125) [B] block. It should pop
into place right under the first.

Since the first servo command is Legs
Stretched (125), set the second block
to position with Legs Standing (45)
(Figure **27**).

5. If you push Button A, it looks like
it should move the servo to 125
degrees, then move it again to 45
degrees. But it doesn't.

That's because the micro:bit is
reading the back-to-back commands
faster than the servo can move. We
need the micro:bit to pause after the
first command — so the servo can
complete its movement — and then
move on to the second command.

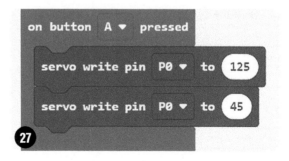

27

Luckily, there's a Pause C block in the Basic drawer. Place a Pause C block after each of your two servo commands so it moves to 125, pauses, moves to 45, then pauses again.

In the digital replica of your micro:bit setup on the MakeCode website, test and adjust how many milliseconds (ms) are ideal for your servo to take its steps. (We find that 250 ms to 500 ms works well.) (Figure 28).

6. Now we want the code to tell our Leopard to take multiple steps after we push Button A.

From the Loops drawer, place a Repeat (4) Times Do D block in the On Button (A) Pressed A block, then add the servo and Pause commands into it. Set the Repeat (4) Times Do D block to repeat the interior code blocks as many times as you want (Figure 29)!

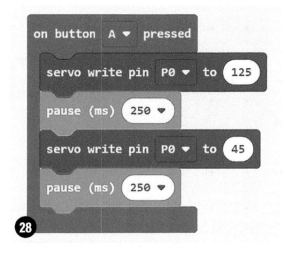

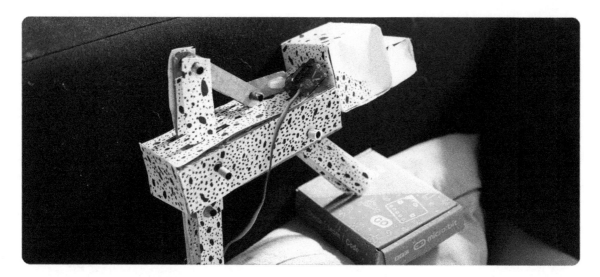

TAKING IT FURTHER

Now that our Leopard can run, it seems like it should be easy to make it walk. But it's actually a little trickier — and takes a lot more code.

The challenge is that servo motors move at one speed, and there is no code block that can change its speed.

So we have to get creative: We're going to break our Leopard's long stride into a lot of tiny movements, with a tiny pause between each one. Strung together, all these micromovements and micropauses will make it seem like it's moving in slow motion.

We'll need a way to add or subtract from the servo's current position, but you already learned how to do that in

chapter 3 (see page 72). Using a variable, we can store and change a number — in this case, the servo position.

1. Open the Basic drawer and pull out an On Start block.

Open the Variables drawer, click on the Make a Variable button, and name it Degrees. Put a newly created Set (Degrees) to (0) **E** block into the On Start block, and set the degrees to the servo's starting position of 125 (Figure **30**). (The On Start block can sit outside of the rest of your code; it just serves to set up a starting position.)

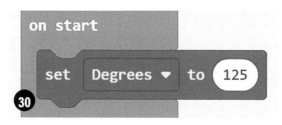

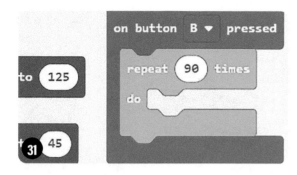

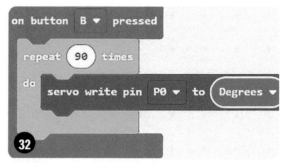

2. Clear out the code in the On Button (B) Pressed **A** block for the Walk code.

We want the servo to turn one degree at a time, and you'll need to do some math to figure out how far it should turn.

In our example, our leg positions are 125 degrees and 45 degrees. Since 125 degrees −45 degrees = 90 degrees, that means we want the servo to move 1 degree and pause, then repeat the loop 90 times.

Open the Loops drawer and grab the Repeat (4) Times Do **D** block, and place it inside the On Button (B) Pressed **A** block. If you change the Repeat number to 90, any code we place inside will run 90 times before the program moves on (Figure **31**).

3. Our first task is to move the servo, so open the Pins drawer (inside the Advanced drawer) and take out a Servo Write Pin (P0) to (180) **B** block and place it in the loop.

Since you've already set up a Degrees (F) variable, drag that code bubble from the Variable drawer and place it in the Servo Write Pin (P0) **B** block (Figure **32**).

4. Now we need to change that variable's value by 1-degree increments. We're going from the larger number (125) to the smaller number (45), so that means we need to subtract from Degrees. Open the Variable drawer again and take the Change Degrees by 1 **G** block and place it into your code.

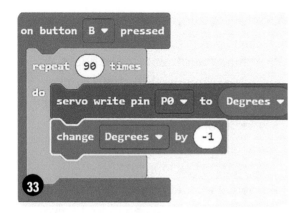
33

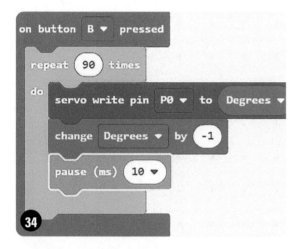
34

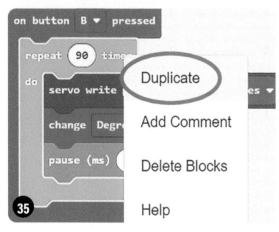
35

If you change the 1 in the text field to −1, then every time the loop repeats, the number used for degrees will decrease by one (Figure **33**).

5. The final task we need to do is add a slight pause between each 1-degree movement. Open the Basic drawer and place a Pause (ms) (100) **C** block under the Change Degrees by (−1) **G** block, and change the pause duration from 100 ms to 10 ms (Figure **34**).

That's about the same amount of time that it takes for a bee to flap its wings twice — too fast to really notice, but slow enough to give the servo a little break.

The testing window should show your servo moving much slower when you press Button B — but only one time, and in one direction.

6. To make the legs slowly move in the opposite direction, we could assemble a similar code combination, but there's an easier way. Right-click the Repeat (90) Times Do **D** block, and choose the Duplicate option from the menu to make a copy of the code assembly (Figure **35**).

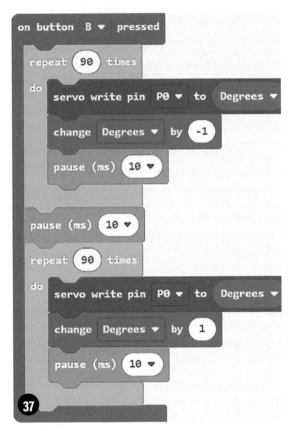

on button B ▼ pressed

repeat 90 times
do
  servo write pin P0 ▼ to Degrees ▼
  change Degrees ▼ by -1
  pause (ms) 10 ▼

pause (ms) 10 ▼

repeat 90 times
do
  servo write pin P0 ▼ to Degrees ▼
  change Degrees ▼ by 1
  pause (ms) 10 ▼

37

7. But we want this command to move the legs in the opposite direction, so change the variable in the duplicate Change Degrees by (–1) **G** block from –1 to 1 so the degrees increase instead of decrease.

Drag this new loop just below the original and add a short Pause (ms) (10) **C** block between them to give the servo 10 ms to move into place (Figure **37**).

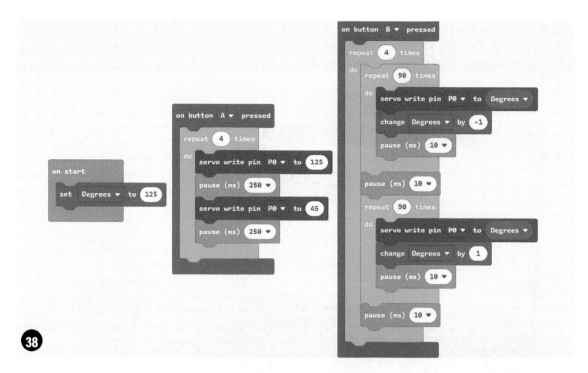

38

8. Finally, add one more giant Repeat (4) Times Do **D** block around the two smaller loops so the entire step cycle will repeat (Figure **38**).

Congratulations: You've just learned a trick for using variables to create a counter, something you can creatively apply to other projects!

AI PETS

You can teach a real pet to respond to human visual commands, like rotating an arm to roll over or lowering a hand to sit. But our Leopard can do that, too!

We've already learned how to use the Teachable Machine's Audio Project to recognize spoken words in chapter 1 and its Image Project to recognize objects like coins for chapter 3. Using its Pose Project, we're going to teach our mechanical pet to recognize gestures and react accordingly.

After learning the basic concepts and training instructions, you'll be able to use your creativity to come up with your commands to customize how you communicate with your pet!

THE TRAINING

In a Pose Project, the AI creates a very simple skeleton of your body using lines for your arms and legs and uses those lines to determine your position and posture. It ignores everything else in the camera view that isn't those lines and dots (Figure **39**).

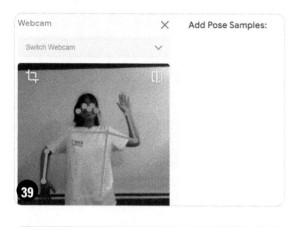

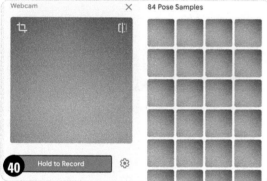

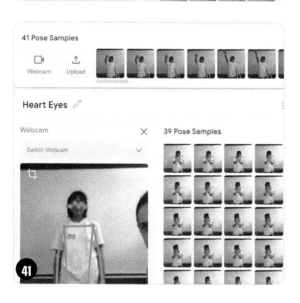

If you train it to recognize different poses, then your creations can react to hand and body movements, just like when you want to train your real pet.

However, body movements are complex: The AI will need more data samples than usual. When standing in front of your camera to take pictures of your movements, make sure you're far enough away that all the lines of the AI skeleton are visible, including your arms, legs, and body.

1. Go to the Teachable Machine website and create a new Pose Project. Make your first class a blank background (Figure **40**).

2. Choose the commands you want to associate with specific movements, and make additional classes with different names (Figure **41**).

   Come up with a pose for each of the commands for Walk, Run, Heart Eyes, Angry Eyes and anything else you've added. Just make sure each pose is different from the others, or the AI might have trouble telling them apart.

3. Once you have your classes trained — and a ton of sample photos in each — it's time to train the AI (see page xxviii). Spend some extra time testing it to make sure all your poses are clearly recognized, adding more photos to the classes that are unrecognizable.

Make sure you add lots of pictures of each pose in different positions (near the camera, far from the camera, at the top of the screen, at the bottom of the screen, etc). This will make sure the AI has enough data to learn each pose. Export your AI model and copy its link (Figure **42**).

THE CODE

Go to makecode.microbit.org and set up a new file, and assemble your starter code from the introduction (see page 107). Add the Teachable Machine's link you just created with your pose classes, and set up each pose. Just be prepared for a very long If statement!

If you're looking for new additions to your Leopard code, look back over previous projects and see what you can incorporate. In our file, we've created three actions: Run, Walk, and Lie Down. We also created Angry Eyes and Heart

Eyes, which create two faces using the micro:bit's tiny LED screen, similar to what we did in chapter 1 (see page 10).

Chase Theme

The Music drawer has a neat block that can make use of a micro:bit v.2 onboard speaker, or you can attach a speaker like you did in chapter 2 (see page 107). Remember: If you're attaching a speaker to your micro:bit, it has to be on pin 0, so you may need to switch your servo motor connection.

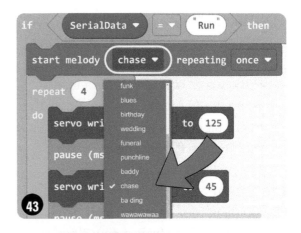

1. In the Music drawer, find the Start Melody (Dadadum) Repeating (Once) **K** block and place it at the top of the If statement that controls the running movement.

2. Click on the first drop-down menu of the Start Melody (Dadadum) Repeating (Once) **H** block, and change (dadadum) to (Chase) — that seems more appropriate for running (Figure **43**)!

3. Click on the second drop-down menu of the Start Melody (Chase) Repeating (Once) **H** block and change (Once) to (Once in Background) (Figure **44**).

Normally, code is read and completed one line at a time, with the program moving to the next line only when

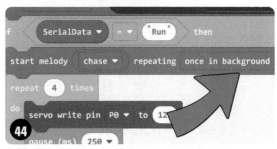

it's finished doing what the code commands so no two commands happen at the same time.

But the Once in Background option enables the program to read and start the first line and then read the next line and begin that action *while the first command is still happening*.

This is a game changer for adding some nice beats to your project!

Want to hear your Leopard roar? Your audio options are limited only by the classes you make and your creativity. Here, we've created a Roar class so when the AI recognizes that pose, the micro:bit plays a tone that simulates a roar (Figure **45**).

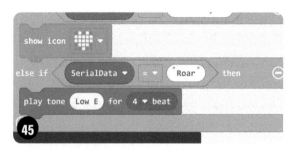

Lie Down

Do you think your Leopard is tired and needs a nap? If you train a new class for Lie Down, you can take a section of code you've already written to make your creation stretch out in the sun.

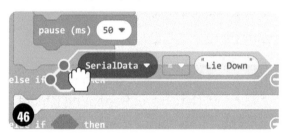

1. A leopard will often stretch with its front legs and back legs out, which happens to be the first movement of our Walk command.

Click on the + icon of your ever-growing If statement to add a new line, and have the SerialData look for Lie Down (Figure **46**).

(If you need a reminder about how to create a SerialData = " " block, see page 107.)

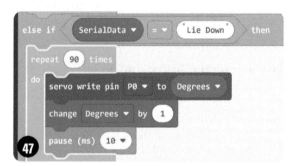

2. Leopards stretch slowly, so you'll want to have yours mimic this motion. Right-click the first part of the Walking loop, which combines tiny movements and pauses, choose Duplicate, and add it to your If statement (Figure **47**).

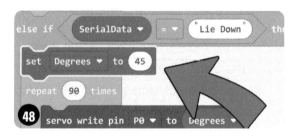

3. Make sure your Leopard is always standing up before you execute this code by adding a Set (variable) to (0) **B** block above your stretching loop, and change the variable to Degrees and the 0 to 45, the "legs standing" position (Figure **48**).

Although you duplicated the whole Walking loop, make sure your Change (Degrees) by (1) block is indeed +1 and not −1; otherwise your Leopard won't stretch its legs outward.

Use the test area of the website to see if your code seems to work correctly, and review your code blocks if something seems out of whack. Sometimes malfunctioning code can just be a matter of a single block out of sequence, or an unadjusted setting. Trial and error is part of every maker's process!

BRINGING IT TO LIFE

Now it's time to download your code into your micro:bit, so head over to the Make: AI Robots website. Connect your micro:bit as usual (see page 21) and copy and paste the link from the Teachable Machine website to add your class datasets.

This project should run fairly straightforward on the Make: AI Robots website, and you should see your AI recognize your pose, and trigger the micro:bit to perform the related command. If you find the AI is having a hard time deciding between poses or chooses too quickly, you may want to adjust the sliders next to the classes to the Stop and Hold function.

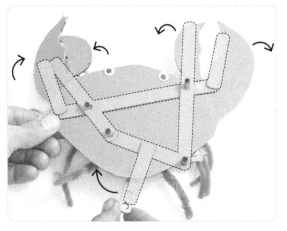

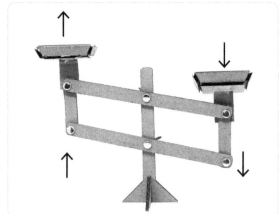

TAKING IT FURTHER

Perhaps a running animal isn't your style. There are plenty of other animals we can bring to life using linkages and your new understanding of how to set up servos, create action code, and train the AI. Check out this Crab that uses a few linkages combined to create real gripping claws!

Or you don't even have to build an animal. Look closely at the world around you; linkages can be used to make any number of fantastic machines. With some crafty use of the linkage bars, you can create working scales, extendable platforms, or even catapults!

And the fun doesn't have to stop with just the servos. Back in the first micro:bit project, you used the LED screen to make faces for Bats and Butterflies. This time,

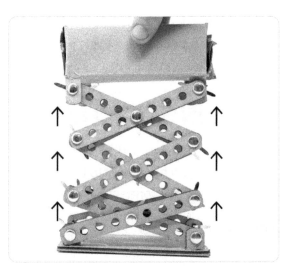

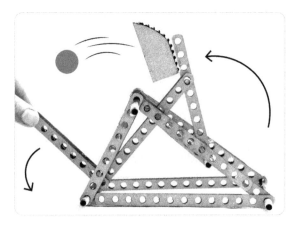

you can use the LEDs to draw eyes for your leopard, but then use your skills to make them blink!

1. In the Basic drawer, find the Show LEDs H block to draw eyes for your pet, and place this in the On Start block.

   Then take an Every (500) ms I block from the Loops drawer and place an empty Show LEDs H block inside, followed by a copy of the LED eyes you just created (Figure **49**).

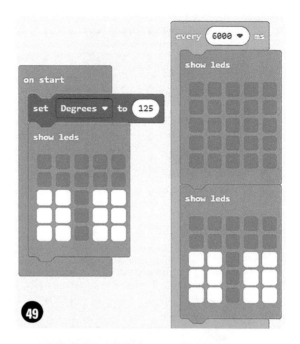

Once you set the timing for the loop (we used 6,000 ms), you can use the testing window off to the side to watch as your creation's eyes blink to life.

Or you can always use these LED eyes to add expressions to your Leopard. You can even use the On Shake from the Input drawer, which senses when the micro:bit gets jostled around. We're pretty sure your Leopard would get angry if you shook it, so draw an angry-looking face on the LED screen and associate it with the Shake input (Figure **50**).

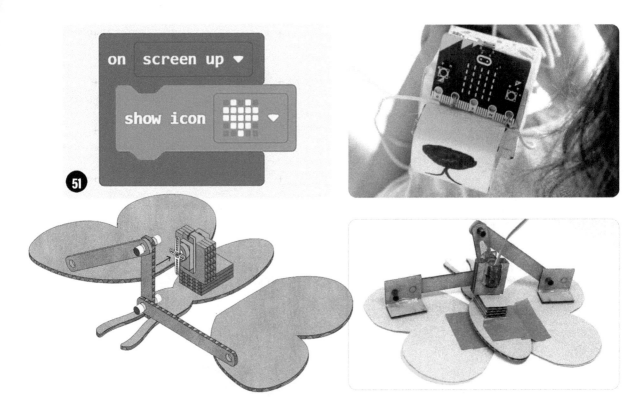

Or what if you held it lovingly in your arms? Is there a way to show that your creation loves you back? The On (Screen Up) block senses when the micro:bit's LED screen is facing upward, and can activate the Show Icon (heart) (Figure **51**).

The loop you made for the blinking animation will eventually draw over these commands, so you don't need to worry about having to use more code to turn them off.

And remember the Butterfly project way back in chapter 1? Linkages are a great tool to help automate the flapping wings. You'll just need to attach a servo to the bottom of your Butterfly, making sure you leave plenty of room for the servo to spin. Then build a small three-bar linkage, glue the center bar to the servo horn, and attach the ends of the other Linkage Bars to pivot points on the wings.

Plenty of other unique animal creations can be brought to life by mixing linkages and AI. Check out this Owl we made! We used the same mechanism as before to make the wings flap, and added a second servo to turn its head to mimic scanning the environment for predators and prey.

You can even train this Owl to make its eyes follow you around the room by training an image-recognition model with three classes: one of you on the right side of the screen, one in the middle, and a final one on the left. Then you'll need a bit of code that will help you turn those servos in the right directions when the AI detects a change.

Add some more code to flap the servo wings every now and then, and you'll have a curious Owl that scans a room and can react to curious visitors (Figure 52)!

```
forever
    set SerialData ▼ to serial read string
    if      SerialData ▼ = ▼ "Left"  then
        set servo P1 ▼ angle to 45 °
    else if SerialData ▼ = ▼ "Mid"   then ⊖
        set servo P1 ▼ angle to 90 °
    else if SerialData ▼ = ▼ "Right" then ⊖
        set servo P1 ▼ angle to 135 °
    ⊕
```

52

Scale

Servo Owl

Micro:bit Leopard

Scissor Lift

Catapult

Leaping Leopard

Fluttering Butterfly

Crab Claws

WRAPPING UP

That's all the time we have to spend on linkages for now. But using what you've learned from these activities, you should have no trouble replicating the linkages you find in your daily life.

We've moved on to more complex designs now that are starting to have more moving pieces, and sometimes that can be a lot to keep organized. Take your time, and don't panic. If you're feeling stuck or frustrated, ask an adult for some advice, or even just take a break; sometimes we need to let our brains reset before we can tackle a problem clearly. Just keep at it with a winning attitude, and remember that mistakes — and learning from those mistakes — are a necessary part of successful making!

Notes:

6

GUMBALL MACHINE

Now that you've built (and coded) some cool projects and developed valuable maker skills, it's important to highlight the most important skill: your imagination.

Maker skills are incredible tools, but they're just tools. The real magic of making is when you add glitter to a butterfly or a spinning bumper to a ball toss, or teach AI to move a mechanical leopard to copy your dog's movements. It's all the weird and wonderful things you come up with on your own, using the concepts you learn in new, innovative ways.

You'll get to flex those creative muscles in this chapter as we build the dispenser box for a Gumball Machine! With this box, you can customize how the machine looks, as well as how it functions. We'll then add motors to replace the hand crank and then use the micro:bit to add a password so only you (and your friends) can use it. Finally, we'll train AI to dish out a treat whenever you enter the room.

CHALLENGE CHECKLIST:

- **Build an internal crank mechanism for a Gumball Machine**

- **Add a motor to spin gears and cranks**

- **Use a micro:bit to add password protection**

- **Teach our machine to recognize faces and dispense gumballs**

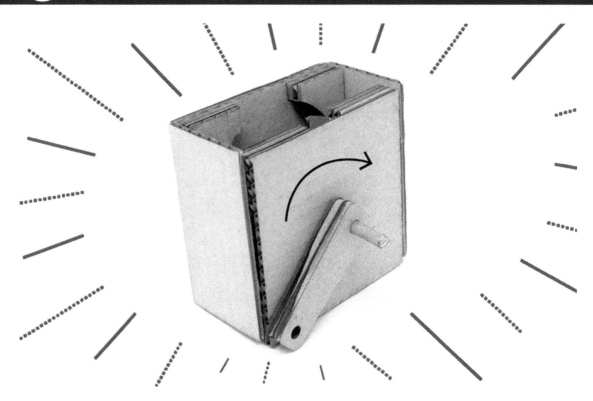

Instead of designing a whole project from start to finish, in this chapter we're going to show you the mechanisms you need for your gumball machine and leave the creative part up to your imagination. The part you're going to be making here is the internal machinery of a gumball machine, a bare-bones model to help you understand what happens inside the machine. Then we'll discuss different ways you can modify this mechanism to fit the various goals of your project.

DISPENSER BOX

Behold the dispenser box! This is a simple mechanism where gumballs sit above the opening at the top of the machine, and when you turn the handle, the wheel inside grabs the gumballs as it spins, dropping them out the bottom. There's not much to it, though putting it together requires a few specific steps. Let's get to it!

YOU WILL NEED:

- Stencils*
- Cardboard
- Hot-glue gun and hot glue
- Scissors
- Hole punch
- Wooden dowel, chopstick, or pencil
- Gumballs!
- Recyclable materials (milk cartons, tissue boxes, etc.)

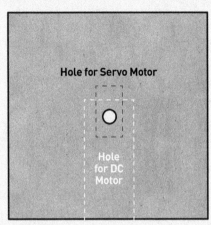

Hole for Servo Motor

Hole for DC Motor

*Wall A (2)

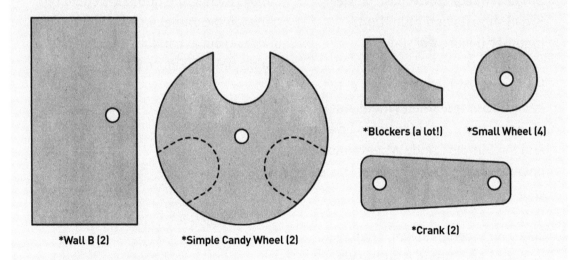

*Wall B (2) *Simple Candy Wheel (2) *Blockers (a lot!) *Small Wheel (4) *Crank (2)

*Download the full-size PDF at makeairobots.com/chapter6.

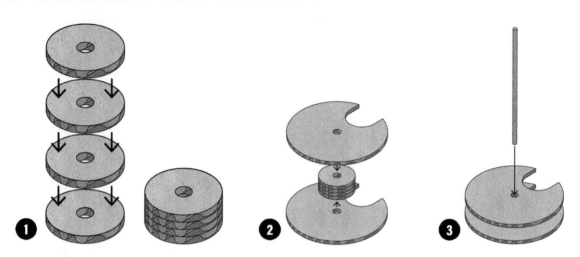

1. Start by tracing, gluing onto cardboard, and cutting the following: two Wall A pieces, two Wall B pieces, two Simple Candy Wheels, and two Small Wheels. Stack four of the Small Wheels and glue them together (Figure **1**).

Position a Simple Candy Wheel to each side of the Small Wheel stack, making sure the center holes line up and the Simple Candy Wheels' oval openings line up (Figure **2**). (This is your "candy catcher.")

2. Take your wooden dowel, chopstick, or pencil and thread it all the way through the middle holes — this serves as an axle. If the axle is a little loose, add some glue so the entire piece will spin as one unit (Figure **3**).

Examine the two Wall A and two Wall B pieces that will form the box that surrounds

the Candy Wheel: What would happen if you just dropped in some gumballs?

Unless they dropped directly into the candy catcher, the gumballs could fall between the wheel and the box walls, dumping out in random directions from the dispenser (Figure **4**)!

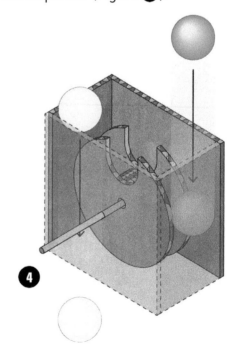

For this project, you want the gumballs to come out in the same spot every time. Imagining how something will work before you glue pieces together is a valuable maker skill to identify potential challenges and refine ideas. In this case, adding a few guide pieces can prevent the gumballs from randomly falling out and increase the machine working as you intend (Figure ❺).

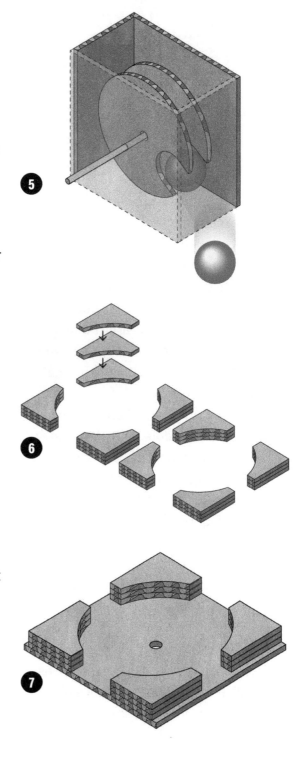

3. This is where all those curved Blocker pieces come in handy. Start by gluing two or three Blockers together (depending on the thickness of your cardboard and the size of your gumballs) in two groups of four (for each corner of your Wall A pieces) (Figure ❻).

4. Line up these stacked Blockers with the corners of the Wall A pieces before gluing them in place (Figure ❼).

5. These blockers create a rail that will prevent the gumballs from rolling out of place. Assemble the walls around the wheel with tape, temporarily affixing them while you assess how everything fits.

If you notice gumballs can still slip through after you've put everything together, add more blockers to each

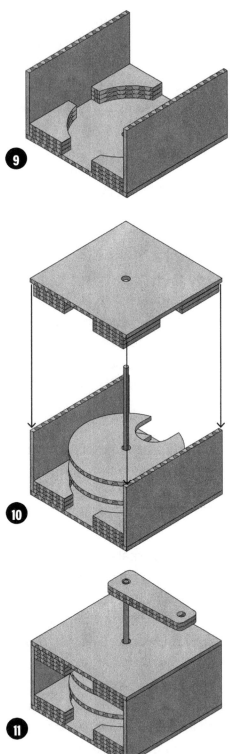

side — just make sure your Candy Wheel can still freely spin (Figure **8**).

6. Once you've fine-tuned the fit, you're ready to create the little case for your Candy Wheel. Remove (or cut) the tape that was temporarily holding everything together and glue a Wall B to both ends of a Wall A (Figure **9**).

7. Slide the Candy Wheel and the axle through the middle hole. With the Candy Wheel in place, you can safely place and glue the other Wall A into place, securing the Candy Wheel inside (Figure **10**).

8. Glue the two Crank pieces together for thickness and slide them onto one end of your axle rod (Figure **11**).

With a bit of glue to hold it in place on the axle, you should have a working dispenser box — all it needs is another piece of chopstick glued into the remaining hole to make cranking easy!

TAKING IT FURTHER

Now that you have an understanding of the mechanism that's used inside the machine, you can design how it looks.

Instead of providing stencils to build the machine's body, we want you to use something from your recycled materials and a bit of imagination. A small box would work perfectly for this project, so scavenge around and see what's available.

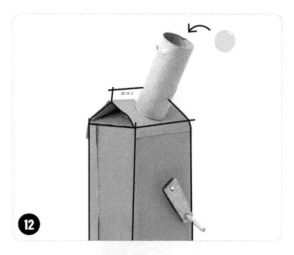

Here's an example of a Gumball Machine we made out of a milk carton. Notice how we made a hole for the axle to go through the side, then glued on the crank handle (Figure 12).

And here's a version using a tissue box, complete with a "viewing window" to show off the internal mechanics (Figure 13)!

And don't let the Candy Wheel's size hold you back — challenge yourself to use all the space inside of a cereal box and build a giant Candy Wheel now that you understand how it works!

You can also focus some of that creativity toward how the gumballs are dispensed. A paper towel roll's cardboard tube works perfectly as a ramp: Cut a large opening on one end of the tube and another opening in the front of your Gumball Machine and slide the tube inside (Figure 14).

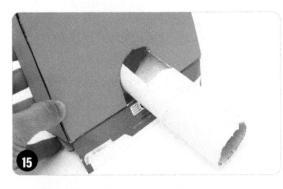

Just make sure the opening you cut in the tube is positioned under the wheel to catch the gumballs as they drop (Figure **15**).

And there are fun things you can do after the gumballs are dispensed, like using some of the concepts and parts from chapter 4's Marble Run so your gumballs go on a journey before they reach you (Figure **16**)!

And the reverse can also work: There's no reason the Candy Wheel can't substitute for a Marble Wheel, adding a steady stream of marbles into your Marble Run.

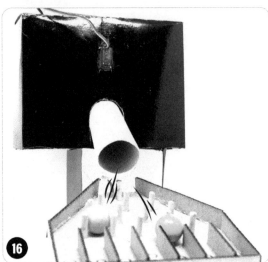

Notes:

YOU WILL NEED:

- Stencils*
- Candy Wheel from the previous project
- Hot-glue gun and hot glue
- Geared DC motor
- Electrical button or switch
- Wires and alligator clips
- Batteries and battery holder

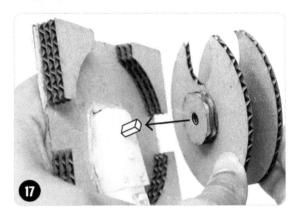

17

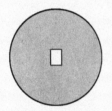

*Motor Support Disc

*Servo Support Disc

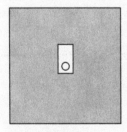

*Hole for Servo Motor

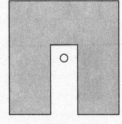

*Hole for DC Motor

*Download full-size PDF at makeairobots.com/chapter6.

There's something rewarding about a hand-cranked contraption. But sometimes it's nice to have electronics to do the work for us.

We're going to use a geared DC motor first to quickly get things moving and figure things out. But since that type of motor can't easily connect to a micro:bit, we'll then connect a servo motor to spin your Candy Wheel to prepare it for adding a micro:bit (Figure **17**).

THE BIG SPIN

The larger DC motor really is the champion for this job. It has a lot more torque, the amount of rotational force that a motor creates, which enables it to spin the Candy Wheel with more power.

This build will be the same as the dispenser box we built in the first section, with two minor changes. You can either take apart the project you made in the previous section or trace new parts and start from scratch (Figure **18**).

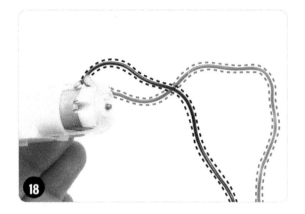

1. Rebuild the Candy Wheel, but this time, glue together two Motor Support Discs from the Stencil Library and attach them to one side of the Candy Wheel. This will create a deep hole for the motor's white end to be inserted (Figure **19**).

    It's important that you line up the small rectangle on the Motor Support Disc stencil (this is for the motor's small white part that spins) with the axle hole on Wall A. You want to make sure that everything is level and not crooked inside the machine.

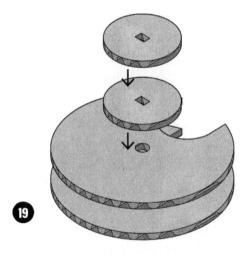

2. Before adding the Wall A pieces, use the Hole for DC Motor stencil from the Stencil Library to trace and cut out a spot for the motor to be embedded on the backside of your dispenser casing.

    Insert the motor, and use hot glue to keep it in place (Figure **20**).

3. The Candy Wheel should connect with the little white knob on the motor. Give a slight push on the cardboard so it connects with the Motor Support Disc you glued on earlier (Figure **21**).

There should be a bit of space between the motor and the wheel. If it's too loose, add a few dabs of hot glue in the hole to secure it. Be careful not to let the hot glue stick to the motor, though, or else it won't go anywhere.

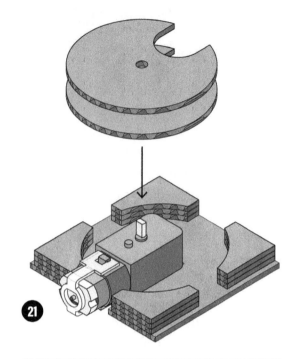

21

4. Your wooden dowel should be the last thing to put in place. Insert it through the hole in the front and through as much of the Candy Wheel as you can.

It should go as deep as it can, stopping when it touches the motor end on the other side. Add some hot glue to secure it in place (Figure **22**).

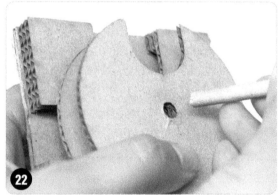

22

The Candy Wheel should be supported from both sides now — from the motor and the axle — and, using wires to connect it to a battery, it should spin. And spin. And keep on spinning?

Let's add some control to our wheel through a button that can turn the wheel on and off. But what kind do you want?

Do you want one that operates like a light switch (Figure **23**)?

23

Or you can try one that will activate the motor only as long as it's held down, like the button we used in the Marble Run (Figure **24**).

For our example, we're going to use a button like we used in the Marble Run, but bigger, and mounted on a simple cardboard frame we made out of cardboard and hot glue.

This big yellow button we use here may look different than the blue button, but flip it over and you'll see that it has the same basic connections you've seen before (Figures **25** and **26**).

This button is great because when you push it down, the wires inside will connect and complete the circuit, enabling power to flow through the motor. When you release it, the circuit is open again and power can't flow — just like the copper tape circuits you made at the start of this book.

5. This motor needs about 3 V to 9 V to run, so any of the power solutions we've used so far will work.

   But remember that these motors work best when given more than the minimum 3 V that two AA batteries

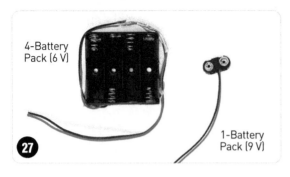

4-Battery Pack (6 V)

1-Battery Pack (9 V)

27

can produce, so we recommend using a three- or four-battery pack or 9 V battery holder (Figure **27**).

6. Once you've selected your power supply, follow the path of the energy leaving the battery. Remember that the red wire is positive, so we need to connect it to one of the leads on our motor. Simply twist the wires together, making sure they won't touch the negative ends (Figure **28**).

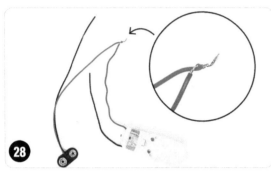

28

7. Now that the motor can receive power, you need to connect the electricity flow back to the battery, with a little detour to the button along the way.

   From the other motor lead, connect a wire to the metal bar poking out of the switch's front. We used alligator clips, but you can also twist the bare wire around the leads (Figure **29**).

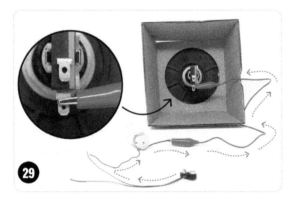

29

8. From the switch's other metal bar, connect a wire to the negative wire of the battery pack (Figure **30**).

   Now when you attach a battery and press the button, the circuit will be completed. With the power flowing through, the motor spins to life as long as you hold the button down and will stop when you let go!

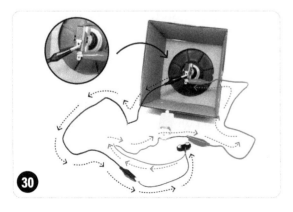

30

TAKING IT FURTHER

You can also use a smaller servo motor, but it's important to identify the type of servo you have.

If you use a **positional servo**, the Candy Wheel can rotate only about 180 degrees. It will drop only one gumball at a time, and you will have to spin the servo back to refill it.

If you use a **continuous servo**, the Candy Wheel can rotate in full circles. This will enable it to load a gumball and dispense it, and continue the loop.

Before moving on to assembling your Gumball Machine with a servo, you need to make a few modifications (Figure **31**).

1. Use the Hole for Servo Motor stencil from the Stencil Library to trace a hole for a servo in one of the Wall A pieces. Make sure the dotted-line circle on the stencil lines up with the axle hole on the other Wall A to ensure that the Candy Wheel will sit properly (Figure **32**).

YOU WILL NEED:
- Stencils*
- Cardboard
- Hot-glue gun and glue
- Scissors
- Servo motor
- Large servo horn with attachment screw
- Servo tester
- Wires and alligator clips
- Batteries and battery holder

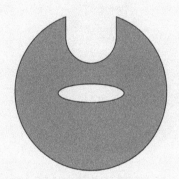

*Servo Support Disc

*Download full-size PDF at makeairobots.com/chapter.

31

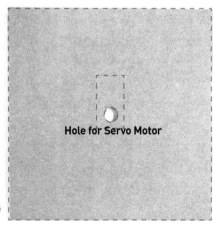

Hole for Servo Motor

32

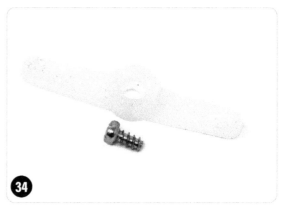

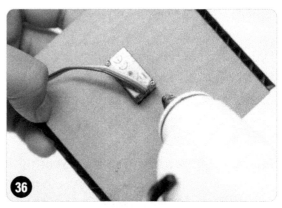

2. You also need to cut out and glue one Servo Support Disc to a new Candy Wheel, also making sure it's aligned to the middle of the wheel (Figure **33**).

3. To connect the servo to the Candy Wheel, you need a large servo horn that has an arm on both ends, as well as a tiny screw that should have come with the horn (Figure **34**).

4. Secure the horn to the top of the servo, and secure it in place by carefully tightening the screw.

Insert the servo horn into the Servo Support Disc, and add a little bit of hot glue to secure it. Be careful not to get any glue between the horn and the servo case, or it may prevent the horn from spinning (Figure **35**).

5. Insert the servo into the hole in the Wall A you modified in and secure it in place with glue (Figure **36**).

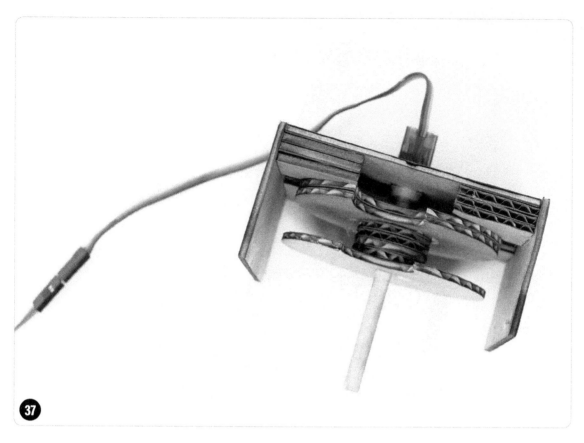

37

6. Finish by placing your wooden dowel, chopstick, or pencil axle as far into the Candy Wheel as you can and securing the wheel inside the dispenser box (Figure **37**).

You don't need to worry about wiring in a button; just hook up a servo tester and connect a power source, and you're ready to place your dispenser in a gumball case.

Servos have less torque than our yellow DC motors, and therefore less strength, so be careful about sending heavy objects through it. Choose the motor that works best for the project you have in mind.

YOU WILL NEED:

- Micro:bit and USB cable
- Computer with internet access
- Continuous servo or positional servo
- Alligator clip–to–male connector pin cables

Find starter and finished micro:bit code for guidance at: makeairobots.com/chapter6

We're going to start explaining projects in less step-by-step detail than in previous chapters, so review earlier micro:bit chapters if you need a refresher course on how specific blocks work the process of syncing your micro:bit. By exploring the earlier projects, you're ready for bigger ideas!

Though you may have had a lot of fun using the yellow DC motors, you'll need to prepare a servo-powered dispenser box in order to code with the micro:bit.

CODE LIBRARY

A — Servos
continuous servo `P0 ▼` run at `50` %

B — Servos
stop servo `P0 ▼`

C — Basic
pause (ms) `100 ▼`

D — Text
`" "`

E — Text
join `"Hello"` `"World"` ⊖ ⊕

F — Logic
`0` `= ▼` `0`

G — Text
length of `"Hello"`

H — Text
`"this"` includes `" "`

I — Servos
set servo `P0 ▼` angle to `90` °

J — Math
`round ▼` `0`

K — Math
`0` `÷ ▼` `0`

L — Pins
analog read pin `P0 ▼`

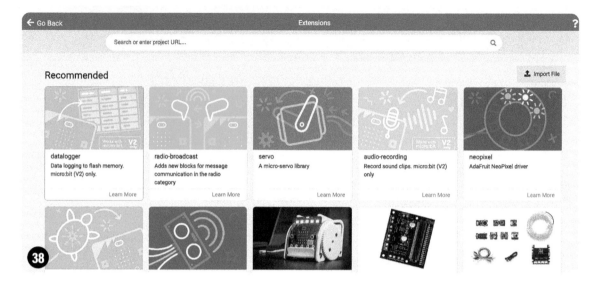

← Go Back   Extensions   ?

And up until this point, you've needed only a positional servo in your micro:bit projects, but we *finally* have a great opportunity to use a continuous servo. But unlike when pairing a micro:bit with a positional servo, we need to add an extension to our project to incorporate a continuous servo.

Start a new project at makecode.microbit.org, and click on Extensions in the list of drawers (Figure **38**).

A new screen will pop up that has a bunch of extra code functions that can be instantly added to your project. Most of these aren't useful to us without a specific project kit, but click on the choice called Servo. This will add a new drawer to your library called Servos.

These blocks function just like those you've already used in the Pins drawer, except now there are separate blocks for each type of servo.

(The Servos drawer needs to be manually added every time you start a new project, so remember this step for future projects!)

CONTINUOUS SERVO

To code the Candy Wheel to spin, grab a Continuous Servo (P0) Run at **A** block from the Servo drawer and add it to a button command from the Input drawer or any other input you want to use.

The number used in to the bubble at the end determines how fast the servo spins, and in what direction:

- If you choose a **positive** number (1 to 100), the servo spins to the right.
- If you choose a **negative** number (–1 to –100), the servo will spin to the left.
- The larger the number, the faster the motor will spin. Run some tests to find the spin you want.
- If you want your servo to come back to a rest, use the Stop Servo (P0) **B** block or set the speed bubble to 0 (Figure **39**)

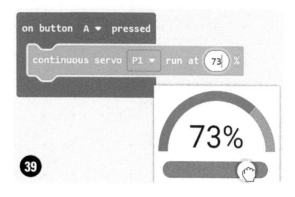

When you test your code, you'll notice the Candy Wheel spin, but maybe the result wasn't *quite* to the position you hoped. That's fine — just change the code and redownload it. Test different combinations of servo speed and pause time to see what works for you!

POSITIONAL SERVO

If you decide to use a positional motor instead, that works, too. Just like with all of your other servo projects, you can use the contents of the Pin drawer.

Positional servos are great if you want your dispenser to slowly give out one gumball at a time. It can rotate only halfway around — 180 degrees — then must turn back to where it started to collect a new gumball.

1. Start by calibrating your servo to 0 in the On Start block. You may need to detach the Candy Wheel and reposition it so it faces the gumball entry point.

2. Tell the servo to turn 180 degrees, use a Pause **C** block to stop it for a little bit so the gumball can unload, and then use another servo block to return the Candy Wheel back to its starting position (Figure **40**).

That's the basics of pairing up a dispenser box with your micro:bit, no matter which type of servo you have!

PASSWORD PROTECTION

With that quick servo lesson out of the way, now you're going to learn how to keep your candy protected from any would-be thieves out there. Using the buttons on the micro:bit as a way to enter a password, you'll be able to activate the servo-powered Candy Wheel only when the correct four-digit password is entered.

While this sounds complicated, if you break this challenge down into smaller tasks, you can see that there are only three main tasks (Figure **41**).

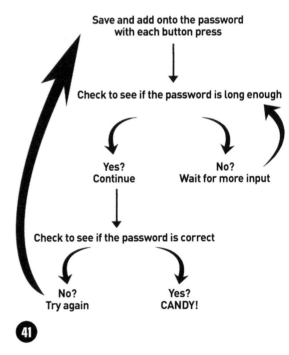

Save and add onto the password with each button press

↓

Check to see if the password is long enough

Yes?
Continue

No?
Wait for more input

Check to see if the password is correct

No?
Try again

Yes?
CANDY!

41

MAKING STRING VARIABLES

Since MakeCode naturally creates all variables as numbers, you'll need to switch the 0 bubble at the end, with the " " bubble **D** from the top of the Text Drawer to save your password as a string of text. With this in place, every time the microbit starts up, the PasswordGuess variable will be blank.

This might sound a little confusing, but even though the password is made up of numbers, we still need to save it as a text string so the code blocks can analyze it one character at a time.

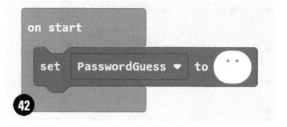

Click on the Advanced drawer, and you'll find the Text drawer. This is where you can find a variety of blocks that enable you to read, examine, and edit any **string variables** that you create. (Strings are just data made up of letters and symbols.)

1. Start by opening the Variables drawer and make a new variable. Make it something easy to remember — in our example, we used PasswordGuess.

Once your variable is created, put a newly created Set (PasswordGuess) to (0) block in an On Start block.

Since MakeCode automatically creates all variables as numbers, you need to replace the 0 bubble at the end with a " " **D** bubble, which is in the Text drawer. This blank " " **D** bubble enables you to save your password as a string of text; with this in place, the PasswordGuess variable will be blank every time the micro:bit starts (Figure **42**).

2. Now we get to the buttons: button A will add a 1 to the guess, and button B will add a 2.

   From the Input drawer, drag an On Button (A) Pressed block into the workspace, and inside of that, add a Set (PasswordGuess) To block from the Variables drawer.

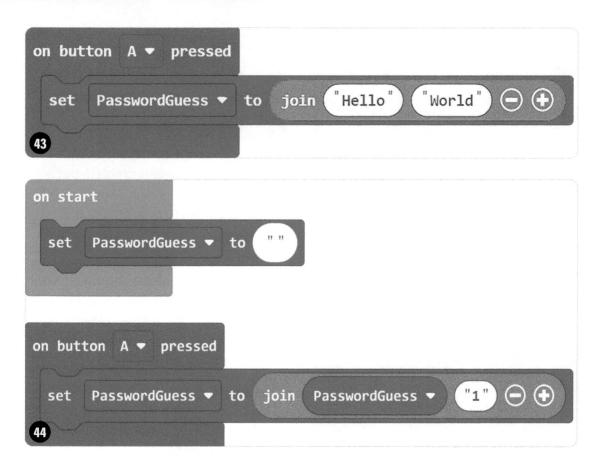

From the Text drawer, take a Join ("Hello") ("World") **E** block and add it to that Set (PasswordGuess) to (" ") block (Figure **43**).

3. Now you just need to tell it what information to join together, which will be our password.

   From the Variables drawer, take a PasswordGuess bubble and use it to replace the Hello bubble. Change World to 1 (Figure **44**).

4. Every time this code is executed, it will take whatever the current PasswordGuess is and put a 1 immediately at the end of that string. Set up button B to do the same, only this time adding a 2 instead.

   This is why we need this variable to be a string instead of a number. With a string, new information is put onto the end of the variable (A + A = AA), but with a number, it will use math and calculate the sum (1 + 1 = 2) (Figure **45**).

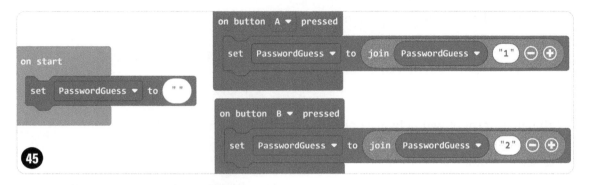

45

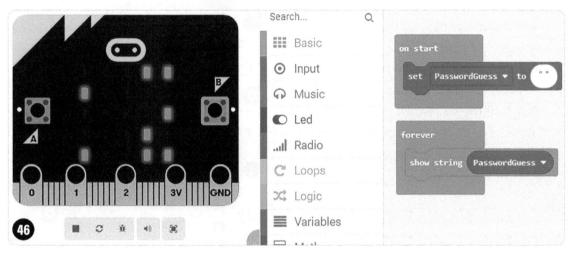

46

5. You can check to see what your current guess is by using a Show String block from the Basic drawer inside a Forever block and adding a PasswordGuess bubble from the Variables drawer to it (Figure **46**).

6. Now it's time to move on to task 2 of the flow chart, where we tell the micro:bit to check how many numbers or letters were used.

From the Logic drawer, place an If statement into the Forever block and a 0 = 0 **F** Comparison hexagon onto the If statement.

From the Text drawer, take a Length of ("Hello") **G** bubble and add it to the first spot in the 0 = 0 **F** Comparison hexagon. Replace the ("Hello") bubble with a PasswordGuess bubble from the Variables drawer. Change the second bubble in the Comparison hexagon to 4 (or whatever length you choose your password to be).

Now whatever code you place in this If statement will activate only when PasswordGuess has four numbers in it.

Notice how we clicked the little + symbol and moved the Show String block into an Else statement at the very end? Reading the code out loud, it says "If the password guess is four digits long, do this . . . ; otherwise, show the password guess on the screen" (Figure **47**).

7. The final task is to actually check that the four-digit guess matches your super-secret passcode. We use 2112 here, but you control which password activates your code.

Start by going back into the Logic drawer and adding a new If statement *inside* the If statement you just set up. Open the Text drawer and look for the hexagon that reads ("This") Includes "(" ")" **H**. Use this hexagon to replace the ("True") in our new If statement (Figure **48**).

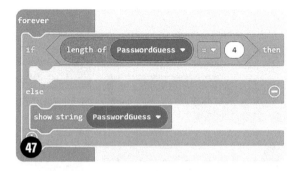

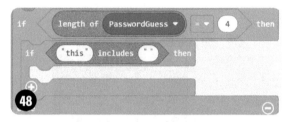

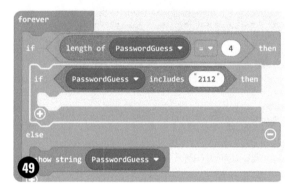

8. Your code will now look at the first bubble ("This") and determine whether it is the same as the string in the second bubble (" ").

All you have to do now is replace the ("This") bubble with a PasswordGuess bubble from the Variables drawer, and enter 2112 (or your own password) into the second bubble (Figure **49**).

9. That checks off the last task you needed to complete. If the password is correct, then whatever you put inside this If statement will be activated. If it is incorrect, it will not activate your inserted code.

Flip back a few pages and copy the servo code from earlier into the If statement to spin your Candy Wheel and release a prize! And since you've gotten so good at coding now, why not jazz it up a bit? You could add a little victory song or even an animation (Figure **50**).

10. The final bit to remember is to add a line after running your servos that would reset your PasswordGuess back to an empty string. Use a Set (PasswordGuess) to (0) block from the Variable drawer with a (" ") bubble from the Text drawer. This will reset the machine (Figure **51**).

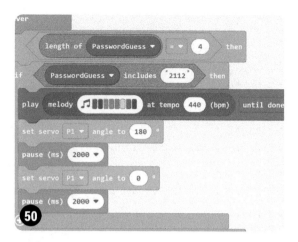

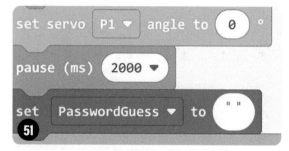

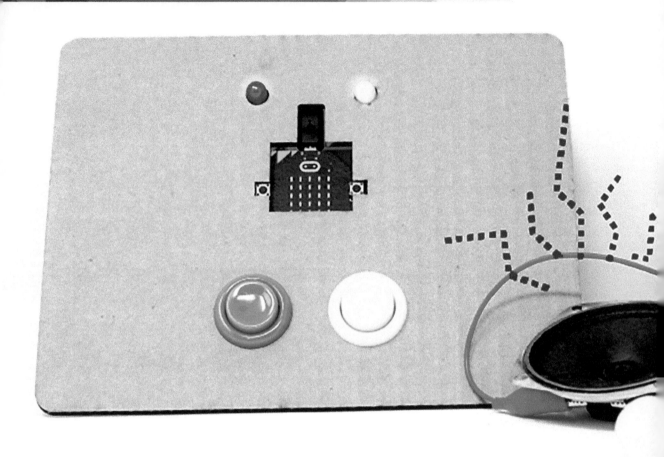

TAKING IT FURTHER

If you want to code what would happen if the password guess is incorrect, click on the second, innermost If statement's + to create an else section. What about adding in a low buzzing noise or a big *X* on the LED screen to indicate the guess was wrong?

Just remember to add another Set (PasswordGuess) to (" ") block under it to reset the PasswordGuess variable so you can try a new password guess.

Once you have your password-protected Gumball Machine running, you can design a case to take it to the next level!

With all the secrecy of our password-protected machines, it's quite easy to see how you could use the AI to enhance this project to new levels of candy protection. Passwords are secure, but sooner or later someone will find them out. Maybe it's a sneaky sibling who is looking to swipe your sweets, or pesky parents who pilfer your popcorn. But if we use an Image Recognition project, we can train the AI to recognize you and only you specifically!

THE TRAINING

Since this isn't your first time setting up an Image Recognition project at the Teachable Machine website, we won't walk through all the set up steps again; if you need a refresher, just look at the AI section in previous chapters. We're going to focus on the important part — making sure the AI knows who you are and has a lot of clear data to work with.

Here are some helpful reminders:
- Did you remember to set up a blank background class so your AI will know what the empty room looks like? Make sure this class just has photos of the scene behind you — no people allowed.

- The class that detects you should have a lot of photos in it. Start with a closeup and move farther and farther back. (You're probably going to need someone else's help to take photos.) Turn to the left and right, jump up and down, and move from side to side to ensure that the camera has an accurate picture of what you look like all over the room — maybe even make a goofy face so no one can cheat by using a photograph of you!

- If there are a couple of people who are allowed to use your Gumball Machine, create a new class for each authorized person and add their photos.

- What happens when a nonauthorized person walks in front of the camera? Does the AI try to think it's you? Consider setting up an extra class called Other People, and take photos of different people in different positions around the room to give the AI something else to consider. This will make it easier for you to code what happens when the wrong person tries to use the machine.

THE CODING

This might be the easiest AI project you will code in this book. Unless you want to add extra functions to your machine, the only task you need to code is to rotate the servo when the AI recognizes you. That code might be a little different depending on what servo you're using in your project (a positional 180-degree servo or a continuous 360-degree servo), but you've worked with servos enough now to have the confidence to know what to do.

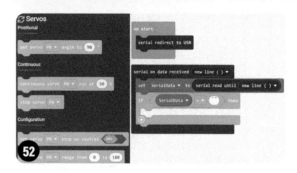

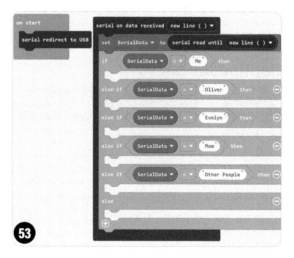

1. Start with a new project at makecode .microbit.org and give this new project a name. Remember to open up the Extension drawer and add the Servos extension whenever you start a new project (Figure **52**).

2. Add all of the classes you trained into the If statement (Figure **53**).

3. Inside each code block, add some code for the servos. We've covered these already in the Micro:bit section, so flip back a few pages to find the lesson there and how you want your Gumball Machine to operate.

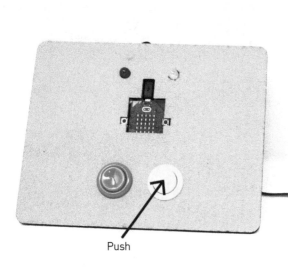

Push

Continuous Servo

Use the Continuous Servo (P0) Run at (50) **A** block, to set your wheel to spin as fast as you want.

If you want the Candy Wheel to dispense only one gumball, you will need to time how long it takes for your Candy Wheel to make one full turn.

Then enter that duration into an added Pause (ms) (100) **C** block from the Basic drawer, and add a Stop Servo (P0) **B** block from the Servos drawer. (The Pause block delays the Stop command long enough for the Candy Wheel to complete its rotation.)

Positional Servo

Place a Set Servo (P0) Angle to (90) **I** block from the Servo drawer into an On

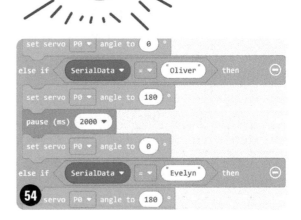

Start code mouth and set it to 0 degrees — this will set the servo to always be facing upward when you turn the project on.

Now in the If statement, add some blocks to tell that servo to turn 180 degrees to dispense a gumball, pause about one second to let the gumball roll out, and then turn back to where it started (Figure **54**).

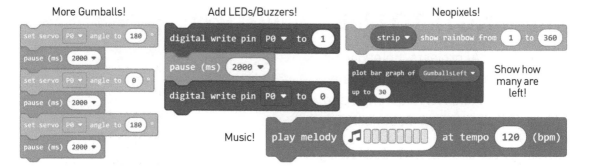

More Gumballs!

```
set servo P0 ▼ angle to 180 °
pause (ms) 2000 ▼
set servo P0 ▼ angle to 0 °
pause (ms) 2000 ▼
set servo P0 ▼ angle to 180 °
pause (ms) 2000 ▼
```

Add LEDs/Buzzers!

```
digital write pin P0 ▼ to 1
pause (ms) 2000 ▼
digital write pin P0 ▼ to 0
```

Music!

```
play melody ♫ ☐☐☐☐☐☐☐☐ at tempo 120 (bpm)
```

Neopixels!

```
strip ▼ show rainbow from 1 to 360
```

```
plot bar graph of GumballsLeft ▼
up to 30
```

Show how many are left!

Don't forget to click the If statement's + to add an else statement, and add some code to warn you when someone who isn't allowed tries to use the machine. You could tie this to a loud buzzer or some LEDs to set off an alarm.

What are some ways you can customize your machine?

Maybe you should code the machine to dispense *two* gumballs when the AI identifies you? After all, you've done all the work and deserve a bonus reward! Or could you add a counter that displays how many gumballs are left in the machine? You could even add a coin stage like the one you made for the Ball Toss game, and start your own business!

When you're done, download your code to your micro:bit and head on over to Make: AI Robots to begin the final step.

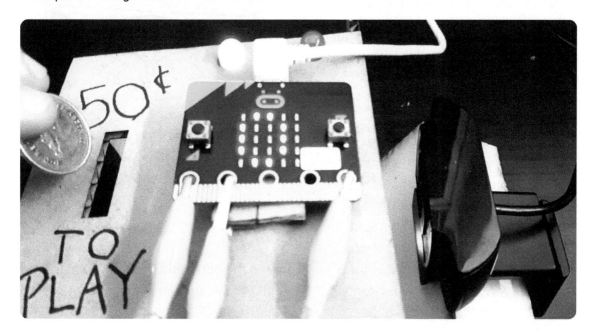

BRINGING IT TO LIFE

As with all our AI projects, upload your AI model from the Teachable Machine website to the Make: AI Robots website at makeairobots.com, and connect your micro:bit.

After starting up your project, everything should be up and running on your Gumball Machine — the servo mechanics, the AI recognition to authorize the gumball drops, and any other customization you added. This project is pretty straightforward, so there's no need to go into settings and change your AI to One Winner or anything like that unless you need to adjust your AI's sensitivity (Figure 55).

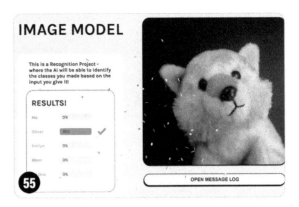

TAKING IT FURTHER

There are a *ton* of possibilities for your gumball machine beyond the basic concepts and components we taught in this section!

Hopper

For starters, you might add a hopper that sits above your dispenser that holds all of your gumballs and helps funnel it toward the opening one at a time. If you're looking at recycled materials, anything that has a slope on it would work well. A milk carton, when flipped upside down, is the perfect shape to

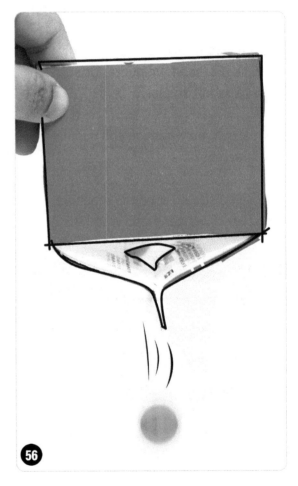

funnel the gumballs into the mechanism — just make sure you wash it out first (Figure 56)!

YOU WILL NEED:

• Stencil*

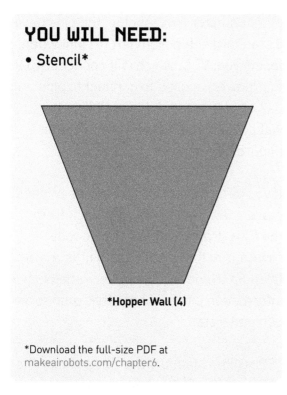

*Hopper Wall (4)

*Download the full-size PDF at makeairobots.com/chapter6.

We've created a Hopper Wall stencil in the Stencil Library so you can build one from scratch if you don't have an empty milk carton (Figure **57**).

Glue four Hopper Walls together to form your funnel (Figure **58**).

If you have an extra paper towel roll, add one to the bottom of your hopper as a stem that leads into the dispenser box (Figure **59**).

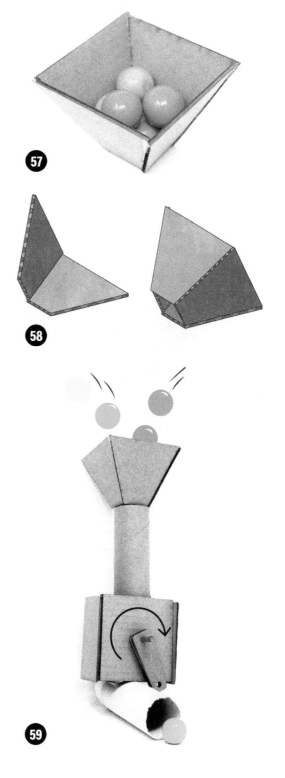

60

61

Potentiometer

Did you know that you can build your own version of a servo tester with the micro:bit and a clever little switch called a **potentiometer**? A potentiometer is a turnable switch that can control your Gumball Machine (Figure 60).

To connect a potentiometer, you'll need three alligator clips. If your potentiometer isn't labeled, the pins have a standard setup from left to right when facing you: VCC, which will connect to 3 V (our power); signal, to connect to pins 0–2 on your micro:bit; and GND, which will connect to GND on your micro:bit (Figure 61).

If you jump into a new MakeCode project, place a Set Servo Angle **I** block from the Pins drawer into a Forever code mouth. You'll need to write a little math formula to convert the potentiometer information into numbers that your servo can understand.

1. Open the Math drawer and look for the Round (0) **J** bubble. Place this into the bubble at the end of the Set Servo Angle **i** block.

2. Go back to the Math drawer and grab the 0 ÷ 0 **K** bubble and place it into the Round (0) **J** block.

3. Open the Pins drawer in the Advanced drawer and look for the Analog Read Pin (P0) **L** bubble, and place this into the first slot of the Round (0) **J** block.

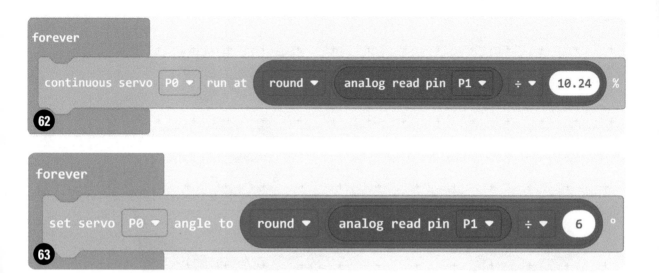

forever

continuous servo P0 ▼ run at (round ▼ (analog read pin P1 ▼) ÷ ▼ 10.24) %

62

forever

set servo P0 ▼ angle to (round ▼ (analog read pin P1 ▼) ÷ ▼ 6) °

63

4. The second Round (0) **J** bubble will change depending on which servo motor you're using.

   For a continuous servo, set the bubble to 10.24 (Figure **62**).

   For a positional servo, set the bubble to 6 (Figure **63**).

Behind the Scenes: Why Those Numbers?

Why those numbers? Let's take a quick look under the hood! Your potentiometer can show numbers from 1 to 1,024. But your servo motor speaks a different number language, which uses 1 to 100 for continuous servos. To make them both speak the same language, we do some simple math: 1,024 (the potentiometer's maximum) divided by 100 (the servo's maximum) equals 10.24. So we set our division bubble to 10.24 and — ta-da! — your servo knows what to do! We made it simple and clean for your robot to understand — no math class required!

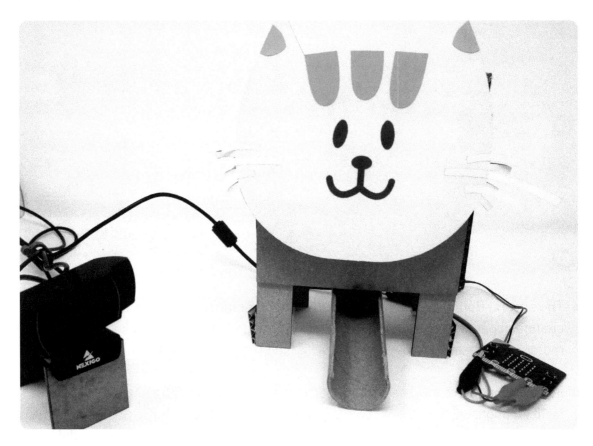

PET FEEDER

Maybe you're looking for a clever way to help a pet with their diet? Using Image Recognition AI again, you could train the AI to recognize your pet instead, and create an automatic feeder!

You would need to modify the Candy Wheel a bit first by adding more blockers to keep the smaller bits of food from falling out.

As far as coding, the continuous servo might be the best choice for this particular project. You may need to spin the wheel a few times to dispense the right amount of treats, so you could add a countdown variable that decreases every time a treat is dispensed so it automatically stops after dispensing the desired number of treats.

WRAPPING UP

You may have noticed that all of our projects now are starting to combine different bits from each chapter. For instance, in this chapter you were able to combine your knowledge of axles with your expertise with servos to open up a world of mechanized creations.

Robotics and AI may seem complicated, but they build on foundational concepts and skills — the same kind of skills that you've been learning. And the more you practice, the more intuitive it will all be.

Creating powerful, complex projects are a lot easier when you break them down into simpler tasks that you already know how to do.

7
SUPERHERO
COSTUMES

Adobe Stock-kegfire, Andrey Popov and QuietWord

Instead of introducing a new cardboard mechanism to use in our creations, this chapter is going to be taking a look at **wearables**, electronic devices that are worn on your skin or clothes.

You might even have some on you right now — a smartwatch or a fitness tracker is considered wearable technology because it analyzes signals from your body and the environment and can display those back to you. Fancy light-up shoes are also wearables, as are VR headsets.

We're going to explore wearables — but of the superhero variety!

First, we're going to make a mask with moving parts to hide our secret identity. Then we'll build a compact shield that uses a motor to spring into action. We'll also learn how to use our micro:bit to energize a power gauntlet, and, last, train an AI to create a target-practice game to refine our aim.

So what are you waiting for? It's time to gear up and save the day!

CHALLENGE CHECKLIST:

- **Build moving masks**
- **Create a spinning Bracer Shield**
- **Code a micro:bit to power up an LED Gauntlet**
- **Use AI to run a Target Practice game**

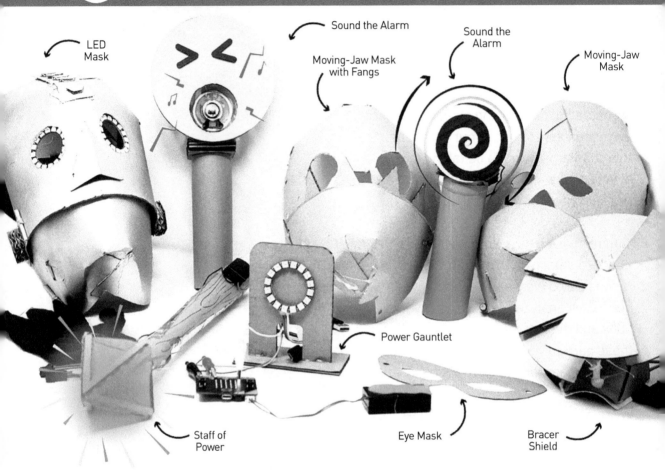

LED Mask

Sound the Alarm

Sound the Alarm

Moving-Jaw Mask

Moving-Jaw Mask with Fangs

Power Gauntlet

Staff of Power

Eye Mask

Bracer Shield

MASK AND ARM BRACER STARTERS

We've included some templates for your costume in the Stencil Library. These are merely guidelines to help you get started with designing your costume, showing basic shapes and ideas. You may need to make them a bit larger or smaller, or change their angles, to fit your face.

While these starting pieces can be worn by themselves, they will also be useful in the next sections as a platform on which to build up our projects.

1. Trace, glue, and cut the Mask and Arm Bracer stencils out of thin cardboard so it can bend with the curve of your face and wrists.

YOU WILL NEED:

- Stencils*
- Thin cardboard
- Glue
- Scissors
- Hole punch
- String or rubber bands
- Elastic band

*Mask

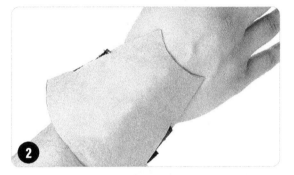

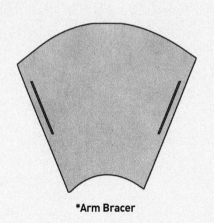

Punch holes in the Mask and use string or a chain of rubber bands to hold it to your face (Figure ❶).

2. For the Arm Bracers, feed the ends of the elastic band through the Arm Bracer slits so they fit around your wrist. Secure the elastic to the Arm Bracer with hot glue or staples; the elastic should provide enough stretch to enable you to remove and put it back on (Figure ❷).

You now have some basic building blocks for becoming a superhero!

*Arm Bracer

*Download full-size PDF at makeairobots.com/chapter7.

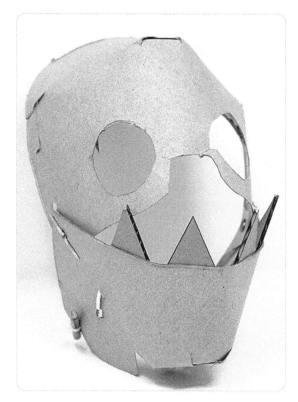

MOVING-JAW MASK

The basic Mask template is great for concealing your identity, but you may want a more radical look. By using our knowledge of hinges and rubber band elasticity, we can create a mask that not only conceals our whole face but also has moving parts!

With this project, you're going to be taking a bunch of thin cardboard and making two parts of a mask that will cover most of your head — one part that covers from your hair to just above where your mouth begins, and another that covers your chin and jaw area. A large cereal box or two works perfectly for this project.

YOU WILL NEED:

- Stencils*
- Thin cardboard, like a cereal box
- Scissors
- Rubber bands
- Brass fasteners
- Wooden dowel or chopsticks

*Download full-size PDF at makeairobots.com/chapter7.

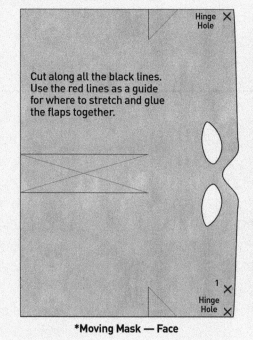

Cut along all the black lines. Use the red lines as a guide for where to stretch and glue the flaps together.

Hinge Hole ✕

Hinge Hole ✕

*Moving Mask — Face

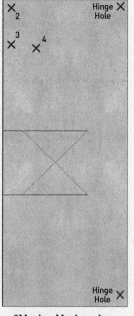

✕ 2

✕ 3 ✕ 4

Hinge Hole ✕

Hinge Hole ✕

*Moving Mask — Jaw

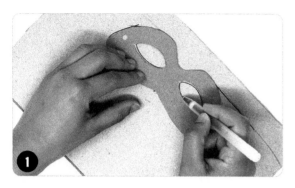

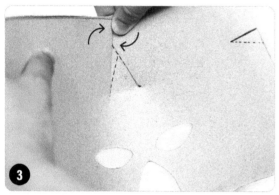

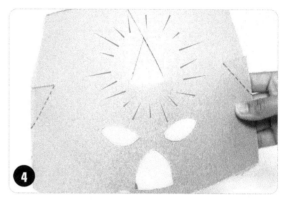

1. Copy the Moving Mask — Face from the Stencil Library onto the cardboard. The solid black lines show where to cut, and the red dashed lines are guides for gluing. (We'll explain a bit more as we get to them.)

   Use the Mask you previously created to properly place the eye holes and nose position (Figure **1**).

2. After cutting away the eye and nose holes, cut along the two black lines that run vertically down the forehead — these will help adjust the curve of the Mask to fit the curve of your head (Figure **2**).

3. Slightly bend one side inward until it lines up with the dashed lines. (You may need to make shorter or longer cuts and bends to customize the curve.) Use hot glue to secure them in place. Repeat with the other side (Figure **3**).

4. Use hot glue to secure the other side, so the top of the Mask curves (Figure **4**).

5. Use the same curving technique on the cut lines on the left and right sides. Cut the solid black line, and fold the top half down and over the cut. Adjust the cuts and bends, and

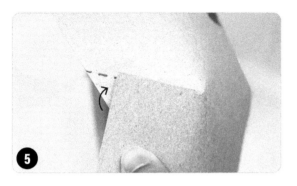

5

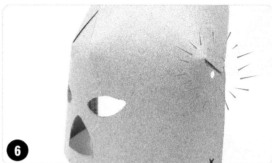

6

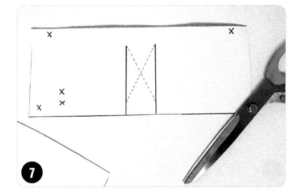

7

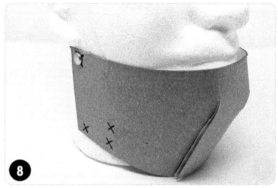

8

glue them in place by the dashed line (Figure **5**).

6. Use hot glue to secure the curves in place (Figure **6**).

7. Copy the Moving Mask — Jaw stencil onto another piece of thin cardboard that is wide enough to stretch across your face from ear to ear and tall enough to cover from your bottom lip to the bottom of your chin.

Cut the black lines and fold the sides to the dashed lines as you did above, forming a curve that fits under your chin (Figure **7**).

8. The area just below the ear is going to be used as the pivot point for the jaw, so make sure your jaw piece is wide enough to stretch all the way across (Figure **8**).

9. Now that you have customized the Face and Jaw pieces to curve to your head, it's time to assemble them (Figure **9**).

Using a hole puncher and these photos as a guide, make several holes on your Mask wherever there is an X on the template. You will need the following holes:

⑨ MASK ASSEMBLY

Upper Mask

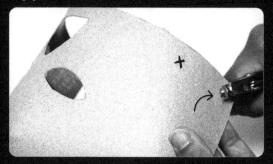 

- One hole on both sides near the bottom corner for hinges

- One hole on the left side, close to where you just made one of your hinge holes, to hold the rubber band

Lower Mask

- One hole on either side near the back of the jaw for hinges

- Two holes about 1 inch apart on the left side of your Mask to stretch the rubber band

- One hole on the left side near hinge hole to hold the rubber band

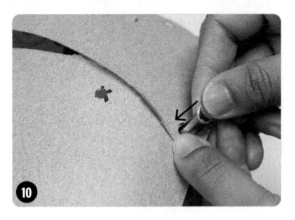

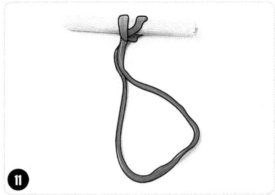

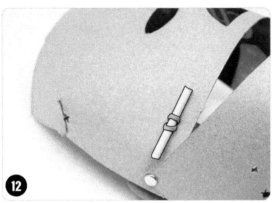

8. Line up the linking holes and connect the two halves with brass fasteners (Figure 10).

9. Take a small piece of wooden dowel and tie a rubber band to it (Figure 11).

10. Thread the rubber band from the outside into the hole in the Upper Mask's left cheek. The piece of wooden dowel will prevent the rubber band from slipping through the hole (Figure 12).

11. Take the rubber band from the inside of the Upper Mask and thread it out of hole 4, then thread it back inside through Hole 3, as if you are sewing (Figure 13).

12. Finally, thread the rubber band back out of the Lower Jaw's corner hold, tying it off on the outside with another piece of wooden dowel (Figure **15**).

Fine-tuning the fit of your Mask will take a bit of testing, but when you open your mouth wide, that movement should push the bottom jaw downward. This movement stretches out the rubber band, and that tension will pull the bottom jaw back up as you close your mouth. A single rubber band on one side of the mask should be strong enough to close the jaw.

TAKING IT FURTHER

Now you can have fun decorating the Mask to match your superhero persona. If you're an animal, add some teeth or fangs. If you're a robot, use aluminum foil to give your Mask a metallic sheen. Or simply use art supplies to add crystals, glitter, and cool symbols like lightning bolts and stars!

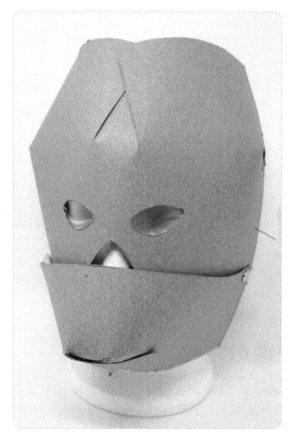

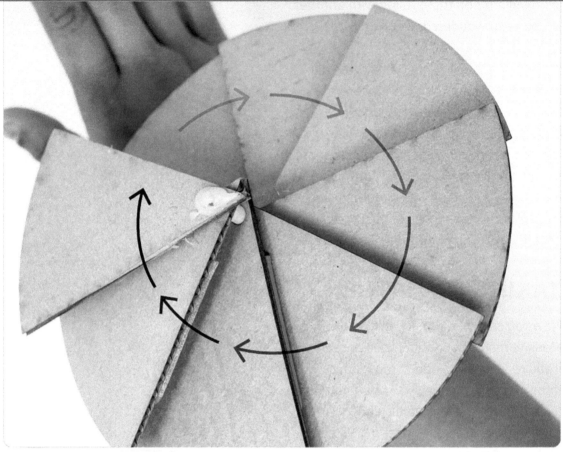

BRACER SHIELD

Now that we've created a mask to hide our secret identity, it's time to create some cool superhero gadgets. But superheroes need to be ready for action, and lugging around big accessories is impractical and they get in the way when not in use. That's where the concept of wearables really shine — having your gadgets on your body is really handy!!

The main job of a hero is helping those in need, and often that means protecting people — and yourself — from harm. The Bracer Shield does just that, appearing when you need to block plasma bolts or ion pulses, and conveniently folding away when it's not needed.

YOU WILL NEED:

- Stencil*
- Cardboard
- Glue
- Scissors
- Hole punch
- Popsicle sticks
- Hot glue
- Wooden dowel, or chopsticks
- String
- Continuous servo motor
- Large servo horn with screw
- Servo tester
- Wires
- Battery
- Plastic bottle cap, like from a water bottle
- Arm Bracer

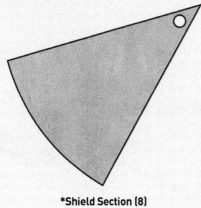

*Shield Section (8)

*Download full-size PDF at
makeairobots.com/chapter7.

1. Print, trace, glue, and cut out eight pieces of the Shield Section.

   Use a hole punch to make a hole near the point of each piece, making sure they're all in the same spot (Figure ⑯).

2. Glue a Popsicle stick down the right-side edge of all eight Shield Section pieces. You may have to cut them to fit (Figure ⑰).

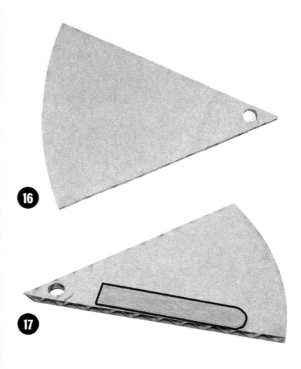

⑯

⑰

3. With the Popsicle stick side up, insert the wooden dowel into one Shield Section and secure it in place with hot glue. This will act as the axle **and** the hinge (Figure **18**).

4. Add the other seven Shield Sections onto the dowel so they spin freely on the axle. Spread them around so each piece overlaps the popsicle stick on the piece immediately beneath it (Figure **19**).

5. Cut the string into 2½-inch pieces.

Starting with the bottom Shield Section (the one that's glued to the dowel), glue the end of the string to the left edge of the cardboard that's farthest away from the popsicle stick.

Firmly stretch the string across and over the next Shield Section. Secure it in place with hot glue (Figure **20**).

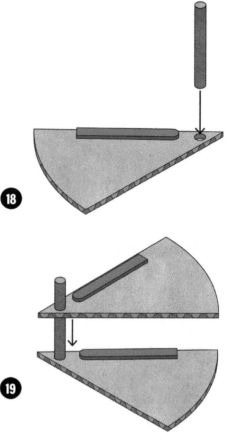

6. Repeat this process, securing a string piece between each Shield Section until all eight Shield Sections are connected (Figure 21).

7. Have an adult puncture a small hole into the center of the plastic bottle cap, just wide enough to fit over the wooden dowel.

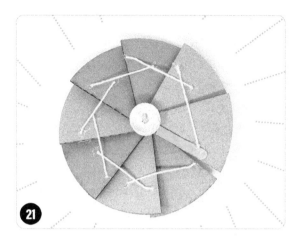

Slide the plastic bottle cap down the wooden dowel until it almost touches the top Shield Section.

Secure the plastic bottle cap to the wooden dowel with hot glue, making sure glue does not drip down between the bottle cap and the Shield Section (Figure 22).

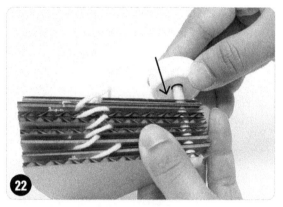

The bottle cap is like a bucket that can be filled with hot glue, ensuring that the two pieces are solidly connected.

8. Cut the wooden dowel above the glue in the plastic bottle cap.

If you turn the top Shield Section, you can see how the Shield Sections will unfold into the full Bracer Shield (Figure 23)!

9. Screw the largest servo horn available onto the continuous servo motor so the horn is secured in

place. Glue the edges of the horn to the bottle cap. Be generous with glue, but always keep watch that none goes inside the servo.

Attach and mount the electrical wires, servo tester, and battery and use the servo tester to adjust the servo's speed and motion so the Bracer Shield smoothly opens. Be careful not to spin the motor too far with the servo tester, or you'll tear the strings from the Shield Sections and need to reglue them.

Once you've fine-tuned the mechanics, secure the continuous servo motor, servo tester, and battery to the Arm Bracer.

The last step is to glue a wooden dowel or stack of cardboard pieces between the bottom Shield Section and the Arm Bracer so the bottom Shield Section doesn't get pulled along with the other pieces.

Now that your basic Shield Bracer is working, focus on the way it looks. Cover the battery and other components with construction paper or thin cardboard, and add paint or colored details to match your costume!

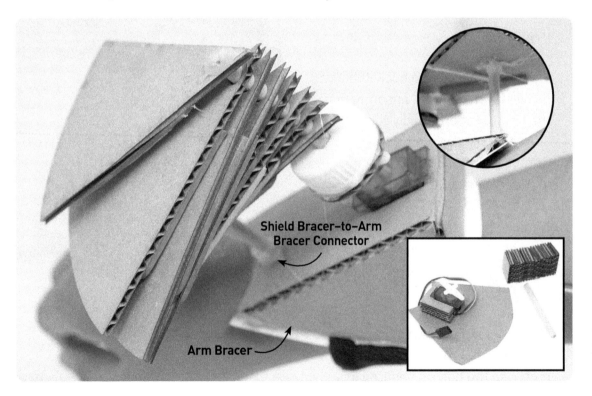

Shield Bracer-to-Arm Bracer Connector

Arm Bracer

Notes:

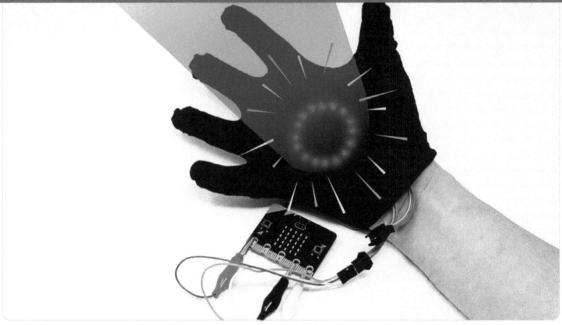

LED GAUNTLET

It's time to get real flashy with our costumes! These activities will be using our favorite add-on to the micro:bit: Adafruit's NeoPixel LED ring. (NeoPixels come in different shapes, like circles and even a grid, so the code blocks refer to them as strips for simplicity.)

These strips of LEDs are a bit more complex than the single LEDs we've been using. The big difference is that each individual LED on the strip can be controlled by a microcontroller — meaning we can not only use our microb:bit to decide things like color and brightness but

YOU WILL NEED:
- Thin cotton or wool glove
- NeoPixel ring
- Tape
- 3 alligator-to-pin wires
- Computer or with internet access

Find starter and finished micro:bit code for guidance at: makeairobots.com/chapter7

also make the colors blink in a specific pattern and timing to animate the lights.

NeoPixel strips require 5 V to run, so you will need a battery pack that can supply

CODE LIBRARY

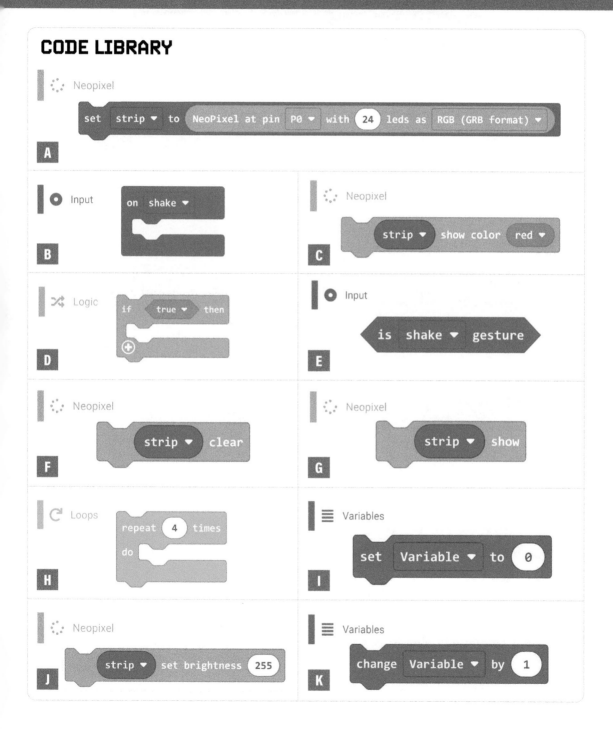

Neopixel

A
set `strip ▼` to (NeoPixel at pin `P0 ▼` with (24) leds as `RGB (GRB format) ▼`)

B
Input
on `shake ▼`

C
Neopixel
`strip ▼` show color `red ▼`

D
Logic
if `true ▼` then
⊕

E
Input
is `shake ▼` gesture

F
Neopixel
`strip ▼` clear

G
Neopixel
`strip ▼` show

H
Loops
repeat (4) times
do

I
Variables
set `Variable ▼` to (0)

J
Neopixel
`strip ▼` set brightness (255)

K
Variables
change `Variable ▼` by (1)

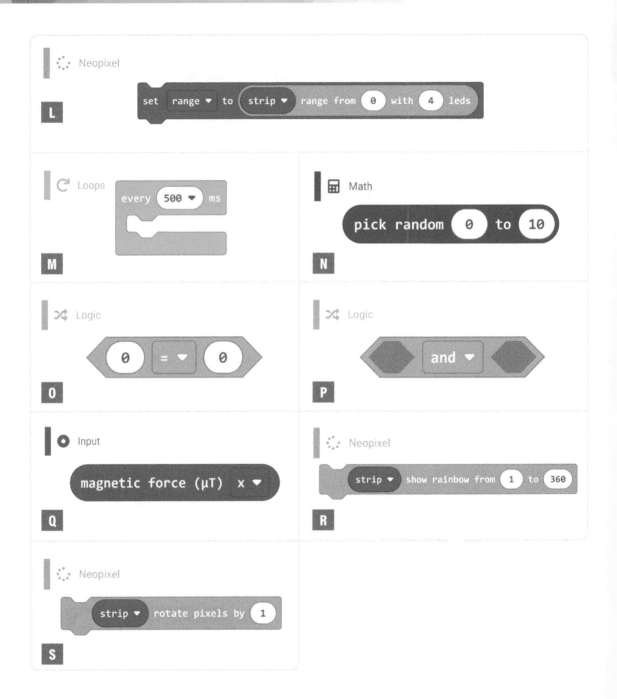

Neopixel

L set `range ▼` to `strip ▼` range from `0` with `4` leds

Loops

M every `500 ▼` ms

Math

N pick random `0` to `10`

Logic

O `0` `= ▼` `0`

Logic

P `and ▼`

Input

Q magnetic force (µT) `x ▼`

Neopixel

R `strip ▼` show rainbow from `1` to `360`

Neopixel

S `strip ▼` rotate pixels by `1`

at least that amount of power. (The two AA batteries that come with the micro:bit won't be enough, but four will.)

The first NeoPixel wearable we will make is a powered glove to go with the Arm Bracer. This LED Gauntlet features a NeoPixel ring in its palm, so the glove needs to be thin enough (or have a loose weave) for the lights to shine through. Once set up, it'll look like it's activating repulsor blasts whenever you raise your hand — with help from the micro:bit.

1. Tape the NeoPixel ring inside your glove's palm with the lights facing outward so when it activates it can be seen through the glove's fabric (Figure **24**).

   Tape the micro:bit to the outside back of the glove, positioning it sideways so the pin connectors are facing your thumb. This is important because we're going to be using the micro:bit's tilt input to activate your lights (Figure **25**).

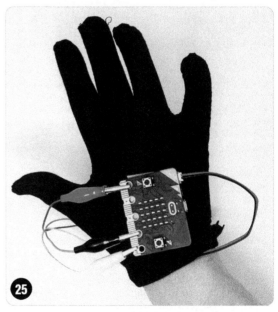

2. You're going to connect three wires between the NeoPixel ring and the micro:bit, like you did with a servo in chapter 6: one positive 3 V electrical wire, one negative GND wire, and one signal wire for communicating with the micro:bit.

The alligator clip should attach to the micro:bit, and the pin end should fit inside the NeoPixel ring's wiring end. (There are two sets of NeoPixel wires, so see the "Connecting Your NeoPixel" sidebar for connection instructions.)

CONNECTING YOUR NEOPIXEL:

- The red wire connects to the micro:bit's 3 V pin (power)
- The white wire connects to the micro:bit's GND pin (ground)
- The green wire connects to the micro:bit's pins 0–2 (signal)

Your NeoPixel ring should have two sets of wires with slightly different ends. Look closely at the back for the tiny label "DIn" (which stands for "digital input," or information coming into the NeoPixel ring) — this is the set you need to connect to your micro:bit.

The wire's pin ends should fit snugly into the end of the NeoPixel ring's wire sets.

(Although not used in this project, the NeoPixel ring's other set of wires can be used to connect a second NeoPixel ring. A micro:bit provides just enough power for two NeoPixel rings.)

Digital Output
Plug into other NeoPixel strips

Digital Input
Plug into a micro:bit

With setup out of the way, now we're ready to dive into the coding. Go to the MakeCode website and create a new project. For this project, we'll do the following:

1. Inside the Advanced drawer, click on the Extension drawer and choose the image labeled NeoPixels to automatically add this extension to your MakeCode library. You will now find the new NeoPixel drawer along the other drawers (Figure **26**).

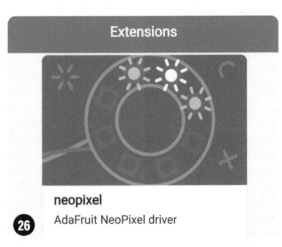

Extensions

neopixel
AdaFruit NeoPixel driver

26

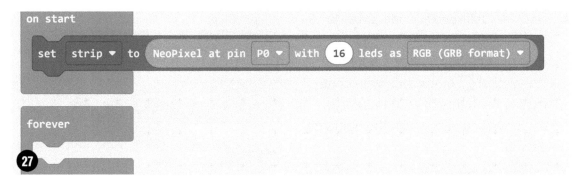

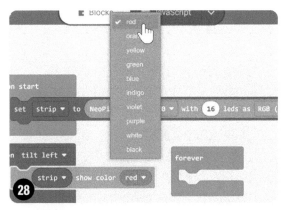

2. Before our micro:bit can talk to the NeoPixel ring, we need to activate them like a variable. From the NeoPixel drawer, drag the Set Strip to (NeoPixel at Pin (P0) with (24) LEDs as (RGB (GRB Format)) **A** block into the On Start block.

   In that block's Pin dropdown menu, select the pin to which you've connected the green wire so the micro:bit knows which pin is connected to the NeoPixel ring.

   Count the number of LEDs on your NeoPixel ring, and enter that number into the bubble so the micro:bit knows how many LEDs are available in the NeoPixel ring. Since we're using these circle LEDS, it should be set to 16 (Figure **27**).

3. From the Input drawer, take an On (Shake) **B** block, which enables the micro:bit's accelerometer sensor to detect movement. Use the block's

pulldown menu to change the input from Shake to Tilt Left so it can detect when you raise your palm.

From the NeoPixel drawer, take a Strip Show Color (Red) **C** block and put it inside that On (Tilt Left) **B** block (or the On (Tilt Right) **B** block, if you have it on your other hand). Set the Strip Show Color (Red) **C** block's color to whatever you prefer (Figure **28**).

Download and test your code. The NeoPixel ring's lights should turn on when you tilt the micro:bit.

4. Now we just need to code a way to turn the light off when your palm isn't raised. We could use another On (Shake) **B** block and write code to turn the lights off, but there's an easier way to easily turn the lights on and off.

   From the Logic drawer, add an If (True) Then **D** block to the Forever block.

   From the Input drawer, find an Is (Shake) Gesture **E** hexagon and add it to replace the (True) bubble of the If (True) Then **D** block.

   Finally, use the Is (Shake) Gesture **E** hexagon's dropdown menu to change the (Shake) option to (Tilt Left).

   This modified block now reads like the On (Tilt Left) **B** block we just made, but constantly checks the If statement to activate the lights rather than doing it once.

   This is a more practical way to turn the lights on and off, so move your (Strip) Show Color (Red) **C** block from the old On (Tilt Left) **B** block and into this new modified If **D** block, and delete the old On (Tilt Left) **B** block (Figure **29**).

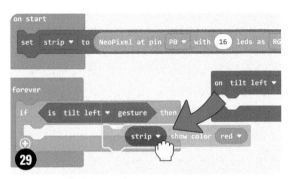

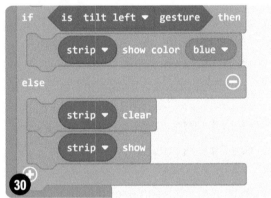

5. Now we need to tell it how to turn the lights off! Click on the + sign at the bottom of the If statement to add an Else statement. This Else statement will essentially say, "If the micro:bit is in any other position other than tilted left, run this other code." (Figure **30**).

   From the NeoPixel drawer, drag both a (Strip) Clear **F** block and a (Strip) Show **G** block into the Else statement.

   The (Strip) Clear **F** block tells the NeoPixel ring to turn off the lights, but only in the NeoPixel ring's internal memory. To get it to show that information on the actual ring, you need to include the (Strip) Show **G** block after the (Strip) Clear **F** block.

Download the code and see if your LED Gauntlet powers up with just a gesture!

Once your LED Gauntlet lights up when you raise your hand, how can we make this effect cooler? In the movies, most superhero tech doesn't just turn on, but slowly gets brighter and brighter as it powers up. We can do that, too! All we need is to create a variable to control brightness and use a loop to slowly increase that variable — just like you've already done in chapter 5!

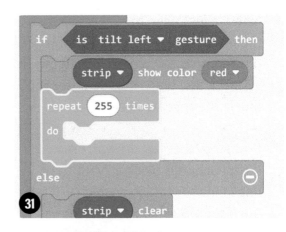

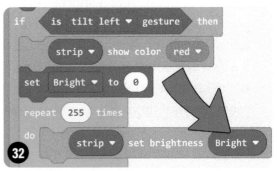

1. From the Loops drawer, take a Repeat (4) Times **H** block and place it just below the (Strip) Show Color (Red) **C** block (which turns the NeoPixel ring's color on in the If statement). Set the loop repeat to 255, the maximum brightness that the NeoPixel ring can safely display (Figure **31**).

2. In the Variable drawer, make a new variable called Bright.

We want this Bright variable to always start at 0 when we raise our hand up, so drag a Set (Bright) to (0) **I** block from the Variable drawer

and place it just above where the repeat loop starts.

Click on the NeoPixel drawer, and just below it you will see a new drawer named More — where you can find even more NeoPixel code blocks.

From this new More drawer, drag a (Strip) Set Brightness (255) **J** block and place it as your first line in the repeat loop. From the Variable drawer, drag a Bright bubble to replace the (255) in the (Strip) Set Brightness (255) **J** block you just added to the loop (Figure **32**).

3. Now we just need to slowly increase the brightness. From the Variable drawer, drag a Change (Bright) by (1) K block and place it as your second line in the repeat loop.

From the NeoPixel drawer, drag a (Strip) Show G block as your third line in the repeat loop, which will tell the NeoPixel ring to display the updated settings. Add a short Pause block from the Basic drawer as your fourth line in the repeat loop, and set it anywhere between 10 ms and 100 ms to have the brightness increase more slowly (Figure ③).

And that's it! Download the code and put the glove on. Test it out to see how well you like it. Remember that you can always go back and change the speed and color; just don't forget to download the code again.

Notes:

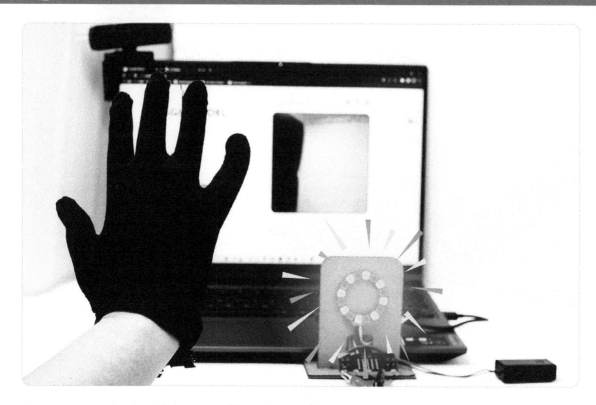

As a costumed crime fighter, you'll need to act fast if you're going to be the hero your city deserves — the LED Gauntlet requires quick reflexes to zap the bad guys.
And just as with math, basketball, and baking, practice is the key to honing your superhero skills, so we're going to make a target practice game to hone your skills.

We're going to program a NeoPixel ring to light up a random section of its ring, and when you hold your hand up toward the correct target, it'll turn green and you'll score a point!

(Since this is just practice, you don't need to wear your LED Gauntlet, especially if you just have one micro:bit and NeoPixel ring and need to use them to run the target system.)

The NeoPixel rings have 16 little LEDs, so we'll create four quadrants as our targets: bottom right, top right, top left, and bottom left. When we train our AI to recognize when you're pointing in the correct direction, it's just a matter of writing code to check whether the two directions match.

When setting up our NeoPixel ring, you might ask yourself, "Where does the circle start?" If you point the wires straight down, the first LED is at the bottom of the ring, moving in a counterclockwise direction. This is why we're going to start with the bottom right as our first quadrant (Figure ③④).

Notice that the first LED in the NeoPixel ring is labeled as 0 instead of 1 — this is how a lot of programming languages define the first "thing," so just remember this when choosing which individual lights you want to turn on.

We made a cardboard display to hold our NeoPixel ring target for the game, but you can also hang it from a hook or tape it to a stand (Figure ③⑤).

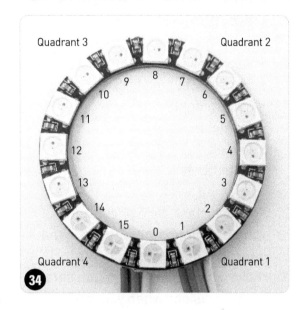

34

THE TRAINING

You need to teach your AI to recognize when we're pointing our project in a specific direction. Let's start off by simply training an AI Vision Recognition Project to tell when we're pointing at these quadrants.

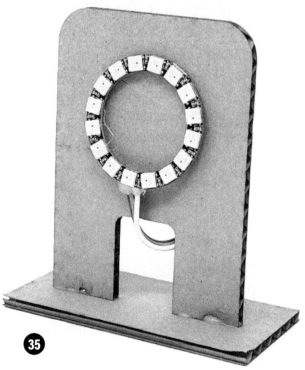

35

1. Go to the Teachable Machine website and create a new Image Project. Set up and train five classes in the same order they'll appear on the NeoPixel ring so they'll be easy to remember. These classes are as follows:
   - StandingStill (the background class)
   - BottomRight
   - TopRight
   - TopLeft
   - BottomLeft

2. For each class, take photos of yourself pointing your device in that direction. Take a lot of photos to make sure the AI has enough data to make decisions when you move quickly — we used about 200 in each category! With each photo, try to slightly move around so there is a range of reference data. Make sure your device is large and clearly visible in the photos. Remember to fill the StandingStill class with pictures of you not pointing (Figure 36)!

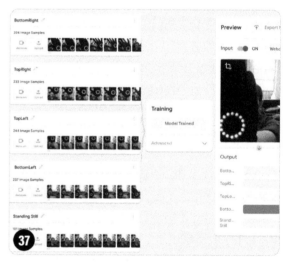

3. Repeat this step for each class, and when you finish, train your AI and test it. You'll want this AI to be a bit smarter and faster than the others you've trained, so you may need to add more and more photos in order for it to run quickly and accurately (Figure 37).

When you're confident that your AI will quickly recognize your movements, export your AI model and copy its link.

THE CODE

Building your own target practice game may seem like a lot of work, but there are actually just three tasks to complete:

- **Setting the Quadrants:** Section off our NeoPixel ring into four parts.
- **Randomizer:** Have the micro:bit choose a random quadrant every few seconds and activate those lights.
- **Coding the AI:** Decide what happens when the AI sees you're aiming in the same direction as the NeoPixel ring's lit quadrant.

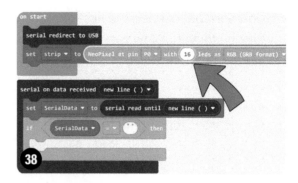

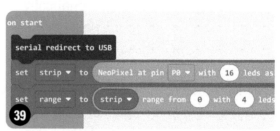

Setting the Quadrants

We're going to start with a new copy of our AI starter code (see page 107), so create a new project and add the NeoPixels extension like we did in the last section.

1. From the NeoPixel drawer, drag a Set (Strip) to (NeoPixel at Pin (P0) with (24) LEDs as (RGB (GRB Format)) **A** block to a Forever block to set up the NeoPixel ring with the micro:bit.

   Make sure to change the number of LEDs to 16 so it matches your NeoPixel ring (Figure **38**).

2. From the NeoPixel drawer, drag a Set (Range) to ((Strip) Range from (0)

with (4) LEDs **L** block and place it as the second line in your On Start block under the code to set up the light strip. This block is just setting up a variable to control a specific set of LEDs on the NeoPixel ring.

The first number bubble tells our group of LEDs where to start, and the second number bubble determines how many LED lights are in the group.

Since NeoPixels start at 0 instead of 1, set the first number bubble to 0 so it will start at the beginning of the ring, and set the second number bubble to 4, so the group contains the first four LEDs (Figure **39**).

This variable defines the first of our four quadrants. Now we just need to set up the other three quadrants.

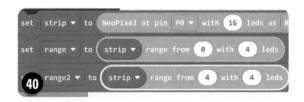

3. Grab another Set (Range) to (Strip) Range from (0) with (4) LEDs **L** block and place it below the other **L** block. You'll notice that each time you add a new **L** block, it will automatically rename it for you to the next one in sequence, in this case to Range2.

Take a look at the NeoPixel ring's numbering photo again and see what the code number for the fifth LED is. Since we count upward from zero, the number for the fifth LED is actually 4. Set that as your first number (the starting LED for the quadrant), and set the second number to 4 (the number of LEDs this group contains) (Figure **40**).

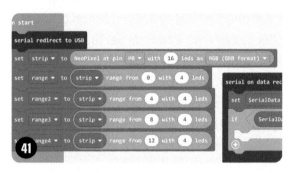

4. We just need two more quadrants now, so add two more Set (Range) to (Strip) Range from (0) with (4) LEDs **L** blocks, and modify their numbers with the pattern we just set up (Figure **41**).

Task one is now complete!

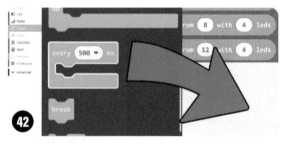

Randomizer

The second task requires us to have the code randomly select one of the quadrants every few seconds. We can easily do this with just a variable and a random-number-generator block.

1. From the Loops drawer, drag an Every (500) ms **M** block and modify the number to how long you want the target to appear; in our example, we chose 5,000 ms (5 seconds) — you can change this number if you want to make your game easier or harder (Figure **42**).

2. Click on the Variable drawer and make a new variable called Target. Drag a Set (Target) to (0) **I** block into the Every (5000) ms **M** block.

Open the Math drawer and find the Pick Random (0) to (10) **N** bubble and put it inside the number value in the Set (Target) to (0) **I** block you just placed. You see those two little number bubbles at the end of the Pick Random (0) to (10) **N** bubble? Change the values to 1 and 4, and each will represent one of the four quadrants (Figure **43**).

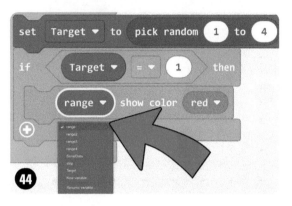

3. With that out of the way, we just need to tell the NeoPixel ring to display the chosen quadrant. From the Logic drawer, drag out an If **D** statement and place it under the random number block. Then replace the (True) hexagon with a (0) = (0) **O** hexagon from the Logic drawer.

If we drag a small Target variable bubble from the Variables drawer and place it in the first spot of the 0 = 0 **O** hexagon and then set the second 0 to 1, we just need to tell the

NeoPixel ring to light up the matching quadrant. This is where the Range variables we made earlier come in — using the If **D** statement, we can link these things together.

You simply need to add a (Strip) Show Color (Red **C** block from the NeoPixel drawer inside this If **D** statement. Click Strip and use the pull-down menu to change it to the Range variable (the first quadrant). Now if the random number selects 1, it knows to light up the first quadrant of the NeoPixel ring (Figure **44**).

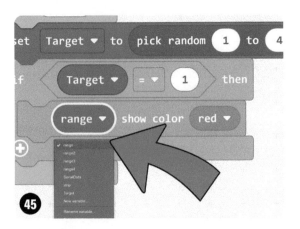

45

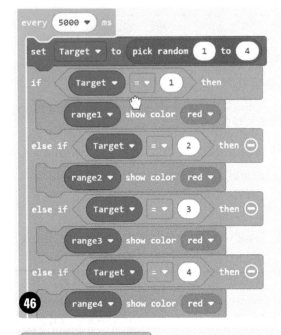

46

47

4. Set up three more parts of this If **D** statement to light up the other three LED groups. Click the + symbol to create more If **D** statement branches, and then right-click and duplicate the Target = 1 hexagon from above and place one into each branch — just change each 1 to 2, 3, and 4 (Figure **45**).

5. Inside each one of these new branches, place a new (Strip) Show Color (Red) **C** block. Remember to once again click on Strip and change it to the correct range you want to use (Range2 for Target = 2, Range3 for Target = 3, Range4 for Target = 4) (Figure **46**).

6. Last, we need to clear off the old light pattern before it chooses a new one, so drag a Strip Clear **F** block and a Strip Show **G** block from the NeoPixel drawer and put them at the beginning of the Every (5000) ms **M** block (Figure **47**).

You've now completed the Randomizer task! You should be able to test this code already, though it won't do much other than switch a group of LEDs around every few seconds.

Coding the AI

Now we just need to add some code to the blocks that listen to our AI.

1. We'll start with the BottomRight class because that's also the first quadrant on the NeoPixel ring.

   We need to check to see if the AI's prediction is the same as the lit quadrant. Take a ( ) and ( ) **P** hexagon from the Logic drawer and place it in the If **D** statement that goes inside the AI code. We'll use this to create some code that is checking to see if SerialData = BottomRight and if the target variable = 1.

   Drag a ( ) and ( ) **P** hexagon and 0 = 0 **O** hexagon from the Logic drawer and use the SerialData and Target variable bubbles to to fill out the blocks (Figure **48**).

   Remember that for this branch of the if statement, we want SerialData = BottomRight and Target = 1.

2. So what should the project do now if you've aimed correctly? Well, that's up to you! With all the awesome coding tricks you've learned up to this point, you should have some pretty wild ideas.

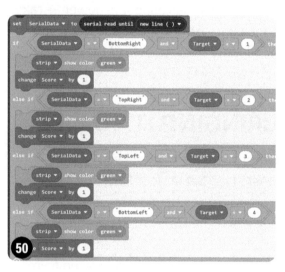

In our example, we've used a (Strip) Show Color (Green) **C** block to turn the whole ring green to let us know we got it right! If you want to make a game out of this, you can create a variable called Score and use a Change (Score) by (1) **K** block in here as well (Figure **49**).

3. Repeat this for each class you trained into the AI, paying close attention not only that the class names match but also that you're using the right Target

to match that group of LEDs on the ring (Figure **50** on the previous page):
- BottomRight is Target1
- TopRight is Target2
- TopLeft is Target3
- BottomLeft is Target4

Now you just need to make sure the NeoPixel ring is connected to your micro:bit and has adequate power — take a look back earlier in the chapter if you need more help, download the code, and you're ready to start.

BRINGING IT TO LIFE

Now comes the moment you've been waiting for. Set up your NeoPixel ring in front of your computer screen so you can see it, use the Make: AI Robots website to pair your micro:bit and paste in the Teachable Machine link you copied from the Training section.

You should now see the lights on your NeoPixel ring's switch around. Move your hand in the direction of the target as quickly as possible. If the AI is able to make a decision before the target changes, you should see the NeoPixel ring change to green and add a point to your score before showing the next target.

If your AI is having difficulty, try allowing it to recognize Standing Still in between your attempts. You can always go back and retrain your model with even more photos so it has more data to learn from.

And remember, this is just the *basis* for a game. We encourage you to take this code and modify it for whatever fantastic projects you can think of next.

TAKING IT FURTHER

Now that you have basic — and advanced! — superhero gear, you can augment your pieces using your craft and electronics skills and imagine new ways to use your micro:bit and AI. Here are a few extra ideas to get you started!

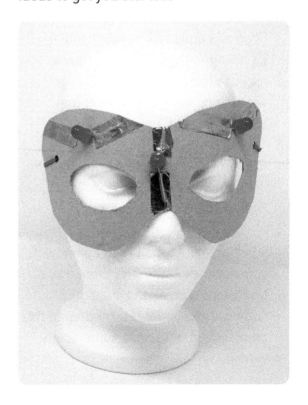

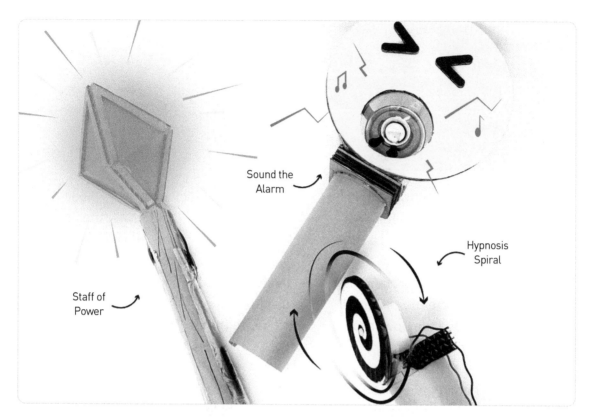

Staff of Power

Sound the Alarm

Hypnosis Spiral

Take your knowledge of copper-tape circuits to add some lights to your Mask or Bracers. Once your circuits are set, use papier-mâché to hide the LEDs underneath. Add a hidden button to secretly light up your superhero costume and amaze your friends!

Or, if your superhero alter ego needs some kind of staff or wand to activate their powers, you can use anything from LEDs to motors or even buzzers and speakers to make an accessory that is unique to you.

If you're using copper-tape circuits to activate your wand, here's a little trick

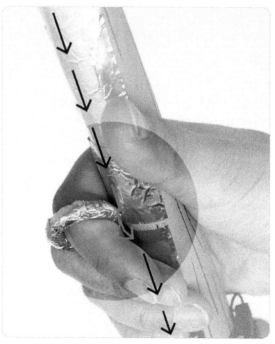

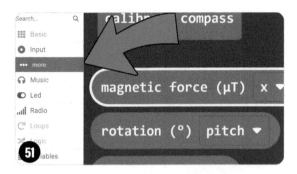

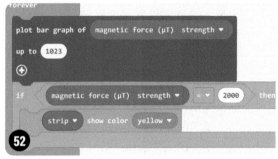

that makes sure it will activate only for you: Take a strip of copper tape and wrap it around your finger like a ring. Now if you leave a small gap in the copper-tape circuit on your wand, your ring will complete the circuit, proving only you have the power to activate your staff!

Looking for something fun to code? Your Shield Bracer could easily be activated by tilting the micro:bit up as well, just like the LED Gauntlet, or by any other of the micro:bit's sensors.

One sensor that we haven't used yet is the **magnetometer**. This gives the micro:bit the ability to detect changes in magnetic fields. The block to activate this sensor is in the More section of the Input drawer (Figure 51).

It's exciting to experiment with the magnet sensors on the micro:bit, especially when combined with the LED

graph block. Click on the Magnetic Force block's small (X), and select the Strength option from the drop-down menu — this will have the micro:bit detect magnets in all directions. The sensor reading will gradually increase as you bring a magnet closer to the micro:bit, indicating the growing magnetic field strength.

If you built an LED Gauntlet from this chapter, hide a magnet in your other glove. When you bring that other glove close to your micro:bit, you can make it "supercharge" your LED Gauntlet, using it to activate commands to change its color or brightness (Figure 52).

Or maybe you're just looking at all those NeoPixel code blocks and wondering, what else you can do? There are plenty of blocks to explore if you're looking to change colors. One of our favorites is the (Strip) Show Rainbow from (1) to (360) R block, which will show you a wheel of colors on your NeoPixel ring (Figure 53).

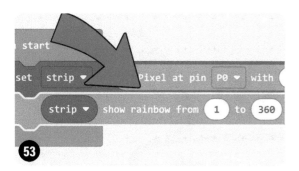

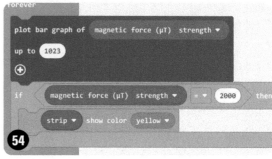

There's even a way to get these colors to spin. If you look at the bottom of the NeoPixel drawer, you'll find the (Strip) Rotate Pixels by (1) S block. Using this will increase the LED position of each color by the number you choose, cycling back to the beginning; remember to use a (Strip) Show G block to actually display these movement changes (Figure 54).

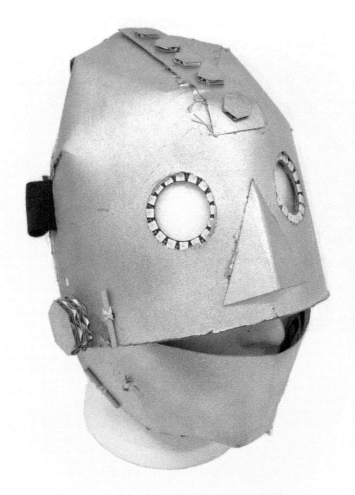

8
ROBOT
FRIENDS

We've come to the final stop on our maker journey together. You've tackled some amazing engineering projects, creating all kinds of cool AI robots. Now it's time to use the experience you've gathered to create something totally unique!

In this chapter, we're going to give you more room to let your creativity soar. Instead of showing you step-by-step instructions on how to make one thing, we're going to show you smaller project ideas to give you inspiration for your own creations. We'll point out some special design features along the way, but not every single construction step, so you can hone your problem-solving skills. It will be up to you to take the pieces you like best and remix them into your very own robot friends!

We've got three mini-project ideas for you: Robot Puppets, Sorting Machine, and Robot Dance Party. For each of these, we'll start you off and provide some basic construction tips to help you on your way, and then show you how to add AI to get your robot friends moving!

CHALLENGE CHECKLIST:

- **Create a robotic puppet that obeys your commands**
- **Build an animatronic animal that watches over you**
- **Construct a sorting machine to help clean your room**
- **Make a robot dance partner that copies your moves**

ROBOT PUPPETS

This first project is probably something you've been looking for in the book this whole time. We're going to create some robotic puppets that will obey your commands!

All of the robots in this chapter use pretty much the same materials, and two servo motors will give them more freedom of movement. If you have only the one servo at the moment, you can still follow along with the projects — use the techniques you learned to compensate for it.

YOU WILL NEED:

- Stencils*
- Cardboard
- Thin cardboard, like a cereal box
- Hot glue
- Servo motors (2)
- Batteries and wires
- Servo horn
- Servo tester
- Micro:bit
- Computer with internet access
- Webcam
- Alligator-to-pin wires
- Straws

*Download full-size PDF at makeairobots.com/chapter8.

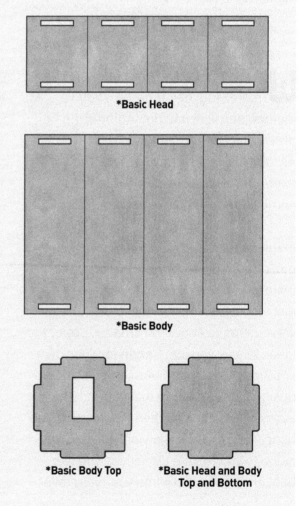

*Basic Head

*Basic Body

*Basic Body Top   *Basic Head and Body Top and Bottom

YOUR FIRST ANIMATRONIC

Have you ever noticed how some robots look and act in realistic ways, like people or animals? You can see these used often in movies and more commonly at theme parks. These are called animatronics — or, more simply, mechanical puppets controlled by lots and lots of electronics (and even more code). While we may not be able to build something as sophisticated as a theme park puppet here, we'll show you the basics of having your puppet look around and open and close its mouth at your command.

In the Stencil Library, we've given you a Basic Head and Basic Body if you need a starting point for your puppet pal, but don't let us get in the way of your creativity — make something unusual or more complex if you're ambitious. Think of what you have in the recycling bin; milk cartons are a great replacement for a body, and yogurt containers could be used to make a head.

When it comes time to make a mouth that can open and close, we'll show you a neat trick with linkages and thin cardboard.

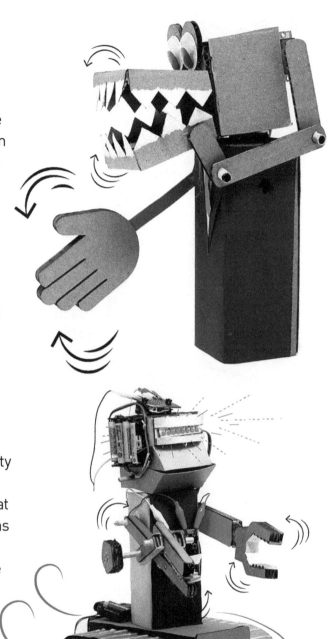

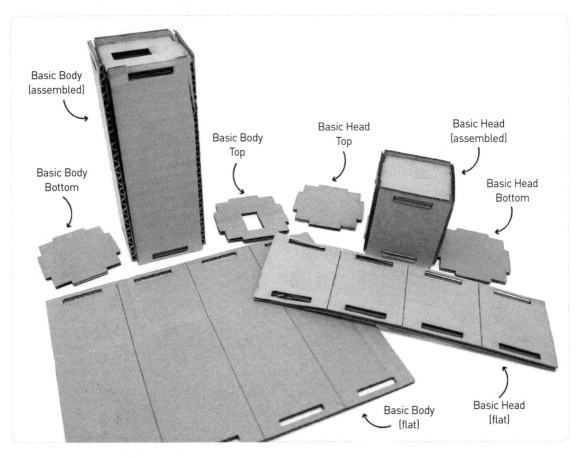

Basic Body (assembled)

Basic Body Bottom

Basic Body Top

Basic Head Top

Basic Head (assembled)

Basic Head Bottom

Basic Body (flat)

Basic Head (flat)

Design and cut a set of jaws similar to ours. The bottom jaw needs to bend where it meets the head, so include some extra cardboard at the back of its "chin" so you can use hot glue to attach it to the bottom of the head. Once that's secured in place, bend the cardboard down slightly where the jaw meets the head to crease the cardboard and make it easier for the linkage to pull the jaw down and then back up again (Figure ❶).

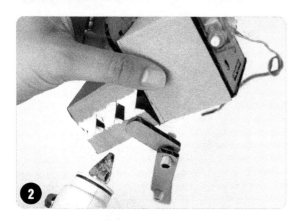

Using a technique similar to controlling the Leopard's tail in chapter 5, create a small three-bar linkage to manipulate the mouth.

You can build a three-bar linkage of any length, as long as one end is secured to the back of the jaw and the other is secured to a servo placed on the back of your puppet's head (Figure **2**).

If you build the jaws using thin cardboard from a cereal box, the servo and linkage should have more than enough power to pull and bend the bottom jaw downward, giving the illusion that your puppet is speaking.

Use a servo tester to see if your linkage works. When the servo spins to point away from the head, the linkage should be able to translate the movement of the servo all the way to the jaw, bending the cardboard downward and opening the mouth as it pulls back (Figure **3**).

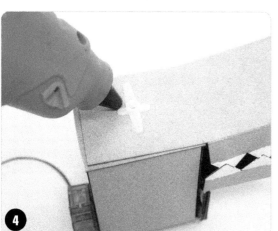

When you're ready to connect it to your puppet's body, glue a large servo horn onto the bottom of the head as centered as possible. Remember, when using glue and servo horns, make sure none gets into the tiny connector hole, or else it can't snap onto your servo after it dries (Figure **4**).

Getting your puppet to turn its head should be simple enough — this is a task you've done many times already. The Basic Body stencil has a built-in spot to hide your motor when making the neck of your puppet. Place the servo motor into place in your puppet's body, using the hollow area inside to hide your wires as they connect to a micro:bit (Figure ⑤).

Finish designing the head and painting it however you'd like. Decorating your animatronic not only personalizes it but is also a good way to hide any excess glue or mistakes (Figure ⑥)!

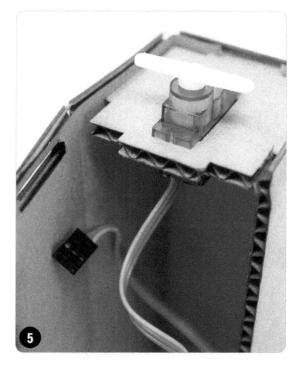

⑤

⑥

Notes:

AI TRAINING

The goal of this project is to have the animatronic puppet copy your head and basic mouth movements. (We're doing open and close with this version, but think about other movements for your next model!) All of this should be able to be done in just four classes: Look Forward, Look Left, Look Right, and Mouth Open.

The Look Forward class will act as our background class for this project, as this will be the robot's default position. Take a bunch of nice close-up photos of your controller — in our example, we're using a normal hand puppet — with its mouth closed. Move it around the screen a little bit so there are multiple reference points (Figure **7**).

Create and fill the Facing Left and Facing Right classes, once again making sure that your controller's mouth is closed in all of the photos. Get lots of good pictures in different positions on the screen for these classes as well (Figure **8**).

For Open Mouth class, open your controller's mouth wide and take a bunch of pictures facing forward, facing left,

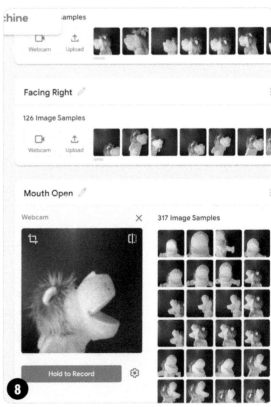

and facing right — but put them all in the same class. This will enable your AI to open the animatronic puppet's mouth regardless of its head position.

Since the Open Mouth class has open-mouthed pictures facing left, forward, and right, it should have about three times as many pictures as the other classes.

It's important to make sure you get a lot of clear, closeup photos of your controller posing in each class. The AI is going to need a lot of data to be able to tell the difference between your Mouth Open class and the other three. You'll know you have a successfully trained model when you can face the controller left and the AI properly predicts it, but when you open your mouth, it will know to switch to Mouth Open (Figure **9**).

If you're having trouble with the AI telling the difference between your mouth open or closed, try putting some tiny stickers on your face as tracking points. When you open your mouth, the sticker will be in a new spot and the AI will have another data point to help it recognize the proper class. This is similar to the motion capture process that turns actors into computer-generated characters (Figure **10**).

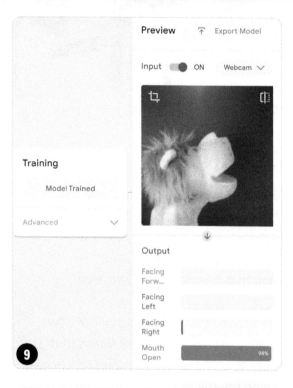

It might take you a few tries to get a perfect model, but it will be worth it when the project is ready. Save your link when you're ready, and then it's time to create some code for these classes.

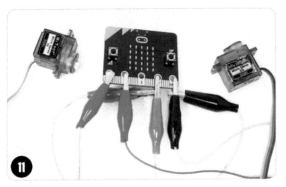

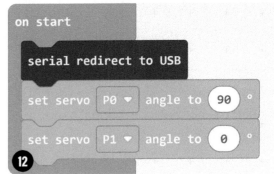

CODING

Before starting your code, think about this project's micro:bit connection. Connecting multiple servos to your micro:bit isn't too complicated — though it does look a little messy.

Using two servos means you have two GND wires and two power wires, but there is only one GND pin and one power pin on the micro:bit.

But that's not really a problem if we're using alligator clips. Just connect the first servo to the micro:bit as usual, and then connect the second servo's GND wire and power wire to the first servo's GND and power connectors (Figure **11**).

This will simply split the signals from the GND pin and power pin between each of those two connections, while the unshared data pins keep the commands separate. But do make sure you have the appropriate servo connected to the right data pin so they operate independently; in our example, the head servo is connected to pin 0, while the mouth servo is connected to pin 1.

Now that the two servos are connected, we can create the code to control each of them.

1. Start with a fresh version of the AI starter code, and go to the Extensions drawer to add the Servo extension to your project.

    From the new Servos drawer, take two Set Servo (P0) Angle to (90) **A** blocks and place them in the On Start block to calibrate their starting positions. Set the first one to P0, and leave the angle at 90 — this block will control the head.

    Set the second **A** block to (P1) and the angle to 0 — this block will control the mouth (Figure **12**).

CODE LIBRARY

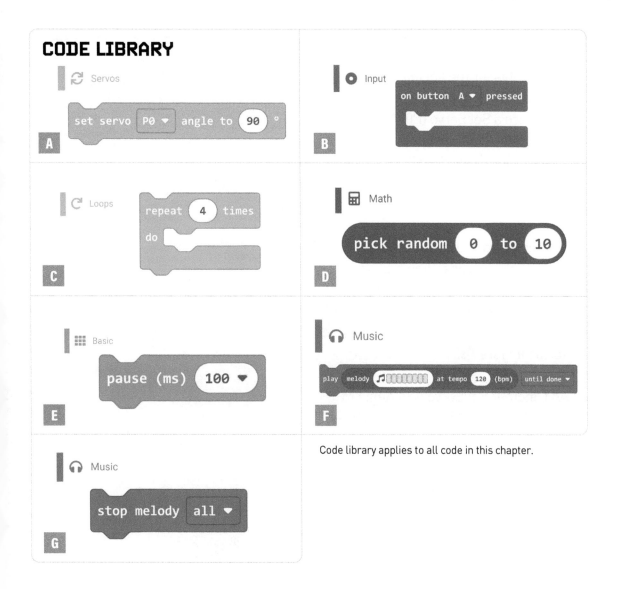

Servos

set servo P0 ▼ angle to 90 °

A

Input

on button A ▼ pressed

B

Loops

repeat 4 times
do

C

Math

pick random 0 to 10

D

Basic

pause (ms) 100 ▼

E

Music

play melody ♪□□□□□□□□□ at tempo 120 (bpm) until done ▼

F

Code library applies to all code in this chapter.

Music

stop melody all ▼

G

2. Now you'll create the code to turn the head left and right. Set up all the If statements for the Facing Forward, Facing Left, and Facing Right classes, and place a Set Servo (P0) Angle to (90) **A** block in each opening. Each of these three **A** blocks will all be set to different degrees to turn the head in different ways.

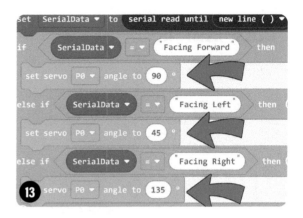

Set the servo in the Facing Forward class to 90 degrees, then add or subtract 45 degrees to turn the head in either direction. Set the Facing Left servo to 45 and the Facing Right servo to 135 (Figure **13**).

3. Add another Set Servo (P0) Angle to (90) **A** block — this time set to P1 — in each of the If statements. Set all three to 0 degrees (Figure **14**).

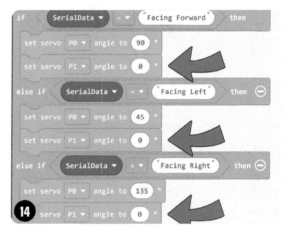

This will close your puppet's mouth, as well as keep the head in the right position every time the AI detects that your mouth has closed. This eliminates the need to train twice as many classes (one for each direction with a closed mouth, and one for each direction with an open mouth).

4. Create a fourth option in the If statement and add one Set Servo (P0) Angle to (90) **A** block. Set it to P1 so it can control the mouth linkage, and

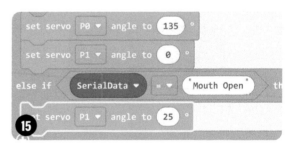

change the degrees to about 25 (Figure **15**).

Since the puppet and its linkage may be a bit different from our example, you'll probably need to tweak this number to determine the best angle.

Head over to the Make: AI Robots website to input your trained AI and connect your micro:bit. The first time you start this project, calibrate your servos by removing the head and placing it back on facing forward, and do the same for the mouth linkage, resetting it so the mouth is closed.

When you've got your puppet pal set up, make sure your controller is in the viewscreen on the right, and your animatronic should spring to life and copy your movements. Congratulations on taking your first steps toward making your own motion-capture studio!

There are plenty of other things you can add to your animatronic puppet, including:

• Servos to move its arms
• LEDs or NeoPixels for eyes
• Music or sound effects from the micro:bit
• Sonar so it can see the world around it.

And you don't need to use a puppet to control your animatronic puppet — try substituting your head as the controller so it mimics your head and mouth movements!

ANIMATRONIC ANIMALS

Another good example of an animatronic puppet is something we introduced in the Taking It Further section of chapter 5. We used our knowledge of linkages to enable the Butterfly project from chapter 1 to flap its wings in a more realistic way, then we mentioned an owl that could flap its wings.

By harnessing the power of AI, we can now make that owl even more lifelike, bringing a new dimension of enchantment to a puppet. We'll train this owl to "follow" you with its eyes wherever you go!

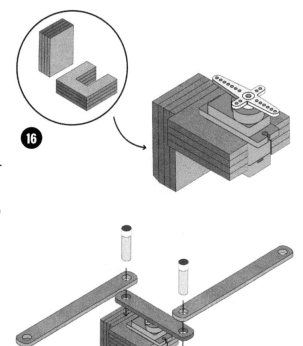

Basic Build

Make sure you design the wings out of a material that can easily bend. Much as with the jaw in the last project, the servo pushes and pulls on the wings to move them back and forth, so consider using thick construction paper or thin cardboard. And just as with the last project, you'll use a three-bar linkage connected to the servo to help the wings move, although in a different way.

Start by mounting the servo to the center of your owl's back — it doesn't matter if it's facing up or down. We connected ours by creating a small U-shaped structure to hold the servo and gluing that piece to

another small group of rectangles to give it some extra space (so the linkage doesn't bump into your owl) (Figure **16**).

Glue a short linkage bar to the servo horn; a five-hole linkage bar should be long enough to do the trick. The other two linkage bars need to be long enough so they extend out from this bar about 1 or 2 inches past the servo structure. Connect the bars with brass fasteners or a wooden dowel (Figure **17**).

Build two small cardboard tabs, and punch a hole in each tab before securing one onto each wing. Use a brass fastener or wooden dowel to attach the tab to the ends of the bars (Figure **18**).

To get the head to move side to side, use the same technique from the Your First Animatronic project earlier in this chapter. Just as in the previous project, use a second servo motor between the body and head to control the head movements (Figure **19**).

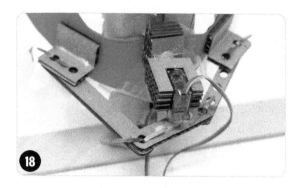

AI TRAINING

Training the AI for this puppet is similar to the last one, only this time you don't need to train a class for the mouth. Because we want the owl to spy on us, instead of facing left or right, actually move to that side of the room when taking reference photos. You may need a second person to take the pictures as you move around the room if you're far from the camera controls. Remember to name your classes something clear, like Left Side, Middle Side, and Right Side.

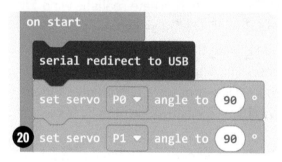

CODING

Hook the servo connected to the head to pin 0 on the micro:bit and the servo connected to the wings to pin 1. Make a new project at the Make: AI Robots website and set up code to control the head. (As a shortcut, you can actually copy and modify the code you used in the last project that moves the puppet's head.)

1. Start with two Set Servo (P0) Angle to (90) **A** blocks in the On Start block, setting the first to (P0) and the second to (P1), but with both angles set to 90 degrees for the owl's starting position (Figure **20**).

2. Set up (or rename) the classes in the If statement to match your AI model: Left Side, Middle, and Right Side.

Place one Set Servo (P0) Angle to (90) **A** block in each opening, and use the same degrees we used in the last project: 45 degrees for Left Side, 90 degrees for Middle, and 135 degrees for Right Side (Figure **21**).

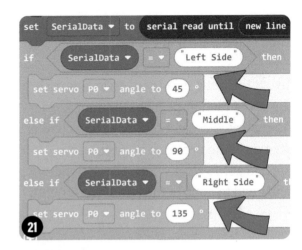

The code to flap the wings doesn't need to be controlled by the AI, so take an On Button (A) Pressed **B** block from the Input drawer and place it next to all of the other code.

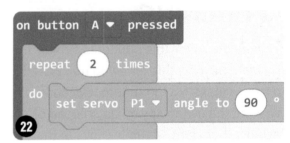

We're trying to recreate realistic wing movement with these servos, so think about what that looks like: Have you ever seen a bird spread its wings and flap them a few times in a seemingly random way? That's what we want to do here.

3. Drag a Repeat (4) Times Do **C** block from the Loop drawer and place it inside the On Button (A) Pressed **B** block, and set it to repeat two times. Then drag a Set Servo (P0) Angle to (90) **A** block inside the loop and set it to P1 (so it controls the wing servo) (Figure **22**).

4. Since real birds are unpredictable, the wing movements of this owl

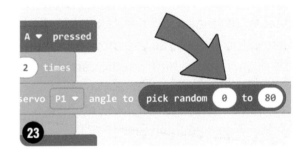

should reflect that; set this servo to turn to a random number.

Open the Math drawer and take a Pick Random (0) to (0) **D** bubble and place it into the degrees slot in the **A** block. Set the range to be between 0 and 80, which will be enough to push the wings forward (Figure **23**).

5. Add a Pause (ms) (100) **E** block set to 250, which will provide time for the servo to move before moving again. Right-click on the Servo **A** block you just made, and select Duplicate from the menu to make a copy of this code with the random number bubble already in it (Figure **24**). (This saves us from having to sort through multiple drawers again.)

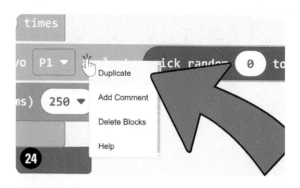

6. Place this new block just below the Pause (ms) (100) **E** block you made, and set the random range of this block as 95 to 180.

The first 0 to 80 range will make the wings move a little bit, then the 95 to 180 range will make the wings move much farther. Add another Pause (ms) (100) **E** block set to 250 at the bottom so the second movement has time before the loop repeats.

Finally, place a third Set Servo (P0) Angle to (90) **A** block after the loop and set it to P1 so the wings return to their starting position (Figure **25**).

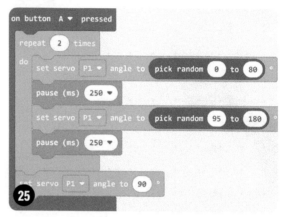

Now whenever you press the A button on your micro:bit, the owl will have a new pattern of flaps to show off!

SORTING MACHINE

One of the most common ideas we hear from kids is a robot that will clean their rooms for them. While that is a little beyond the scope of this book, it is possible to build a robot that will help get the job done: We can train an AI to recognize and sort objects into different buckets.

A common use for AI is to study large sets of data and sort them, and we're really just building a real-world version of this. We'll help you get started, then leave it to you to customize this Sorting Machine for your room.

This is going to be a simple sorting machine that will sort one object at a time. Much as with the coin stage in chapter 3, you'll place an object in the center of the machine. After the AI classifies the object and sends that information to your micro:bit, the servo will sweep the object into the appropriate place and reset for the next object. Grab some containers and find the closest mess you need to clean up, and let's get started engineering a solution to this problem!

YOU WILL NEED:

- Straws
- Servo horn (2)
- Servo motor (2)
- Cardboard
- Hot glue
- Cardboard box
- Pencil
- Scissors
- Tape
- Boxes or basket for the sorted items
- Alligator-to-pin wires
- Servo tester

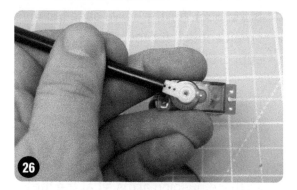

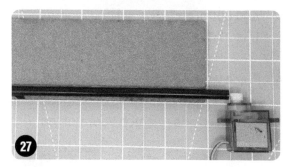

Compared to most of the projects in this book, this one is relatively simple. To start, you'll need a sturdy cardboard box as your workstation. You can also use something like a cereal box, but stuff the inside with something like a towel or books so the box doesn't sag.

1. Start by building the arms of the Sorting Machine that will push our objects to the correct side. Take one of your straws and slide it over the end of your servo horn so it's nice and snug (Figure **26**).

2. Now measure and cut out a rectangle of cardboard that's about as long as your straw, and about 1½ inches wide. Glue your straw to the bottom part of the cardboard rectangle, making sure to position it on the correct side of the straw so it can push objects (Figure **27**).

   Repeat these steps to create a second arm with the other servo.

3. Now we're going to place these arms onto our cardboard workspace. Trace

the bottom of your servos near the bottom-left and top-right corners of your box, which will be holes that are big enough for the servo base but small enough for the servo's upper support to rest above the hole.

Cut out the holes and thread the servos and wires through their new holes, securing the upper supports with a bit of tape. Rotate your servos so these pushing arms sit at the top and bottom of your sorting workspace (Figure 28).

4. Place your Sorting Machine on a flat surface, and place a box or basket on both sides to catch your sorted

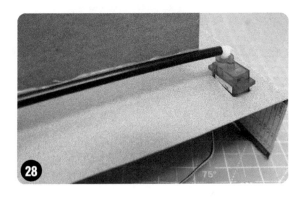

objects when they're pushed off the sides.

Connect the servos to your micro:bit, and remember to connect the servos to separate data pins so they move independently (but split the GND and power pins between both servos) (Figure 29).

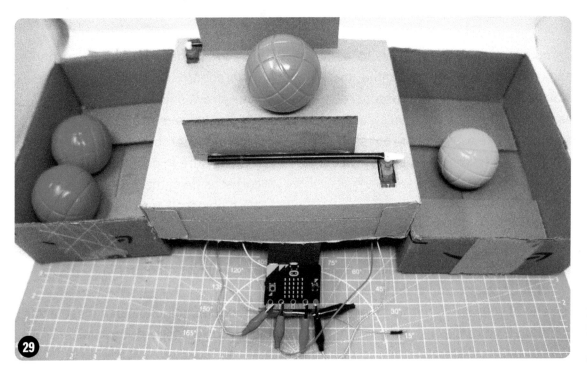

AI TRAINING

Now comes the fun part of the activity: figuring out what you're going to sort. Maybe this is a coin-sorting machine to help you organize your piggy bank, or something to sort little plastic bricks. In our example, we're using the Sorting Machine for colorful balls.

How you want this machine to sort your objects will also determine how you set up your three classes.

If you want the machine to push one object to the left and then everything else to the right, you just need to train an Empty Machine class, as well as Object and Not Object classes (Figure **30**).

If you want the machine to sort two specific objects out of many, train an Empty Machine Class, an Object 1 class, and a Wrong Object class — fill this last class with photos of random objects so the AI can identify when an incorrect object is put into the machine. You will also have to remove any objects from the sorter at that point, or invent a solution like the one at the end of this section, built by our friends (Figure **31**).

When setting up the Image Model, remember to start with an Empty Machine class with nothing on the sorter.

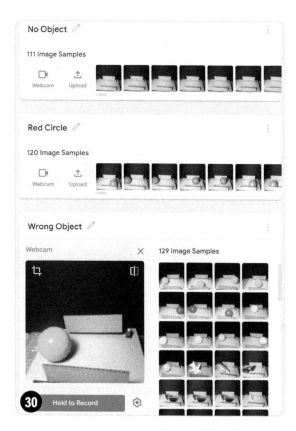

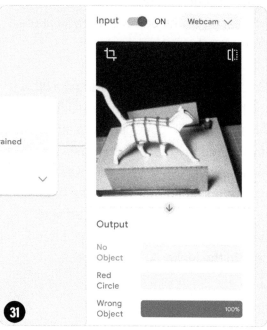

This will help the AI reset between each item.

Next, set up the classes for each item you want the machine to sort. Your webcam should be mounted high so it's looking down at your Sorting Machine, enabling it to clearly see the object when you place it on the workstation.

Rotating the object and moving it a bit each time you take a picture will help the AI know what it looks like from all sides. If you need the machine to make a quick decision, be sure to take lots of pictures of your object so your AI has the data to make a proper decision. You can also tweak the AI sensitivity when you head over to the Make: AI Robots website.

CODING

After saving your Image model link, it's just a matter of coding the servos to do what you want.

1. Set both servos to their starting position of 0 in the On Start block, making sure one is set to P0 and the other to P1 (Figure **32**).

2. Remove and reattach your pushing arms the first first time you start so they're properly calibrated — they

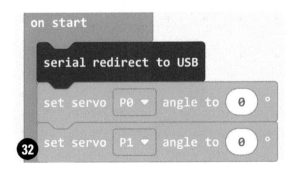

need to be on the top and bottom of the workspace (Figure **33**).

3. After setting up your starting position, set up each class choice in the If statement. Start with the Empty Machine class you trained and put *both* servo blocks there, set to 0 degrees. This will enable the machine to return the arms to their starting point after it has pushed an object to the side.

For each of the other classes you trained, place one of the servo blocks inside and set the angle to 90 degrees so it can rotate and push the object. Be sure that one of your servos is set to P0 and the other to P1.

Add a Pause (ms) (100) **E** block and change the time to 500 ms to prevent the arm from moving back too quickly when the machine no longer detects the object (Figure **34**).

4. You can also use the Show LEDs block from the Basic drawer to add lights to your device: Perhaps use a checkmark when an object is identified, or an arrow indicating

33

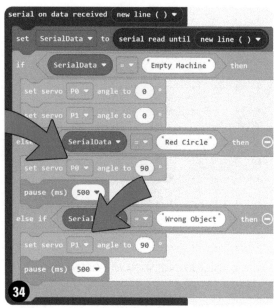

34

which direction the object is being pushed when a class is chosen. If you made a Wrong Object class, you can have a large *X* appear on the screen, accompanied by a sad melody activated by the Play Melody **E** block from the Music drawer.

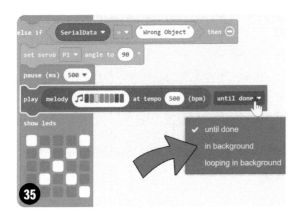

Stop Melody (All) **F** block in the Empty Machine class to reset the sounds along with your servos (Figure **35**).

5. Download this code, and you're ready for the Make: AI Robots website. Input your Image Recognition model link, connect your micro:bit, and have your Sorting Machine help organize your mess (Figure **36**)!

And remember, this concept is just the starting point for your own ideas. Our friends at Strawbees designed a conveyor belt to further automate a sorting machine for their geometric models: A very long sheet of paper is attached in a loop around two paper towel rolls, with motors slowly pulling the objects along.

In our example, they will activate one after another as each block completes its job. If you want music to play at the same time your servo is moving, click on the drop-down menu at the end of the Play Melody **E** block and set it to In Background. This will enable the program to move on to the next lines of code while the song is still playing.

If you select Looping in Background, the melody will continue until you tell it to stop. From the Music drawer, place a

They placed the camera at the beginning of the conveyor belt and used multiple micro:bits to control multiple servo arms along the line. After determining the amount of time that it takes the conveyor belt to move an object to the different servo arms, they used a pause block to delay each servo from moving until an object was in the correct position for sorting.

This is a great example of how the different types of project skills — craft, electronic, micro:bit, and AI — can come together to add a new layer of awesomeness!

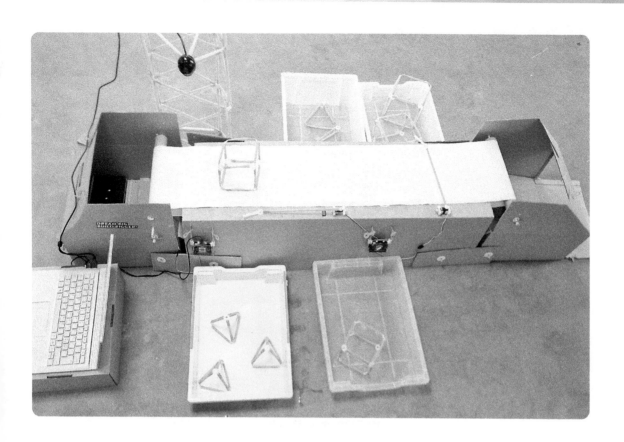

YOU WILL NEED:

- 9-Hole Linkage Bar with holes in 4, 5, and 6 (x2)
- 6-Hole Linkage Bar with holes as you need them (x2)
- Pivot pieces, like brass fasteners
- Cardboard
- Scissors
- Hot glue
- Servo horn
- Servo motor
- Tape
- Alligator-to-pin wires
- Servo tester

ROBOT DANCE COMPETITION

We've done quite a few AI projects in this book that use the Pose Project from the Teachable Machine website. This final project idea will make use of all those silly poses you've come up with and create a robot that can dance with you!

There are really only two things you'll need for this project: servos and linkages. We're going to use the awesome power of linkages and their ability to transform movement in new ways.

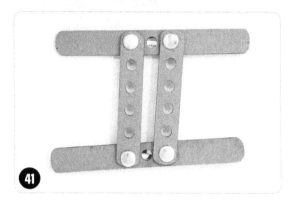

We'll leave the construction of the robot body and design up to you, but the Basic Body and Basic Head stencils can act as a guide if you need a little help.

What we *will* show you is how this little guy works:

1. Using some pivot pieces, connect both 6-Hole Linkage Bars to the 9-Hole Linkage. The first will connect to the 9-Hole Linkage-Bar at hole 4 and the other to the bar at hole 6. Connect the other 9-Hole Linkage Bar at the bottom, and this structure should form a rectangle (Figure **41**).

   This linkage is essentially the skeleton of your robot. The bottom bar will connect to the legs, and the top bar will connect to the arms.

2. Glue a servo horn onto the middle of the top 9-Hole Linkage Bar. Make sure you have a large enough space for these to pop out the sides of your robot as the servo moves it.

   Cut another hole in the upper back of your robot where you can place a servo, and insert the motor so that it spins inside your robot (Figure **42**).

3. With the servo in place, connect the linkage to the servo (Figure **43**).

4. We need to do one last thing to make sure this linkage stays in place. Like we did with the Leopard in chapter 5, we need to create another fixed pivot point to hold the "skeleton" in place as it rotates. The middle hole on the lower 9-Hole Linkage Bar is a perfect spot for this.

   Using a wooden dowel, measure where this fixed pivot will sit, and create a hole in the front and back of the body so the pivot can slip all the way though. Use tape or glue to keep it in place and your creativity to hide it from sight (Figure **44**).

5. Now finish up by connecting arms and legs of your own design to the linkage bars sticking out of the body's sides.

   Since this dancer is going to be jittering around, it may not be able to stand up on its own. Create a stand that can hold your robot upright while it dances around.

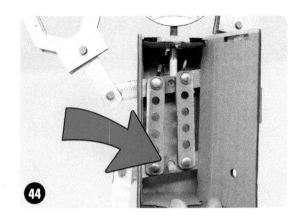

44

Add on whatever artistic bits you want to give your dancer some personality!

With just a servo and a servo tester, you could set it to auto mode and let your robot dance in a loop until your batteries run out. And if you connect a micro:bit to this project, you can program different dance moves or sequences at the touch of a button.

But we're here to show you some fun with artificial intelligence, so we're going to use the Teachable Machine website to train an AI to recognize some of your own dance moves for the robot to copy.

If you've had a chance to play around with this linkage mechanism, you've probably noticed the simple dance moves we're going to train for the AI. Nothing fancy here, just a happy dance where you jump from foot to foot and wave your hands in the air — just like the robot we've designed as an example. The Pose Recognition model works perfect for this, since it will be easier for the AI to tell where your arms and legs are.

1. Start a new class and name it Standing Still. This is that background class that you are now a master at creating. Make sure it sees that your legs are straight and your arms are at your sides (Figure **45**).

2. One class should be called Hop Left, and the other should be Hop Right. Train both of these classes with enough data so the AI can make a quick decision — like the project in chapter 7, you want the AI to make lightning-fast predictions. Take photos in different areas around the room, because who stands in one spot to dance (Figure **46**)?

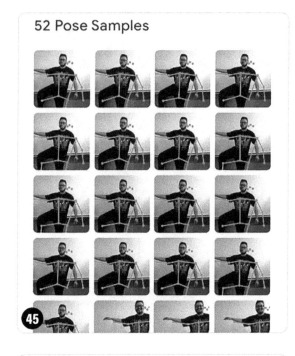

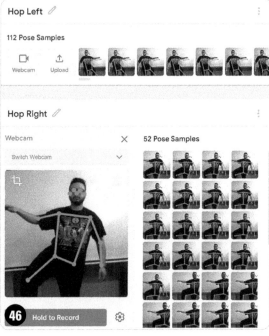

CODING

There really isn't anything too difficult when it comes to coding this project; you've done a lot of work with servos already. Open up a fresh copy of the AI Setup code, and we'll code a little boogie.

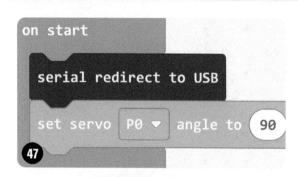

1. In the On Start block, use a Set Servo (P0) Angle to (90) A block to calibrate the servo as you start it up. Set this to 90 degrees (Figure **47**).

   Reset your linkage bar by popping it off the servo and reconnect it so it sits parallel to the ground on startup.

2. The only two If statements you'll need to code are the Hop Left and Hop Right classes, and each needs a single Set Servo (P0) Angle to (90) A block placed inside.

   The servo doesn't need to be turned much — only about 25 degrees in each direction from its starting position — so set one block to 65 degrees and the other to 115 degrees.

   For the Standing Still class, set the resting state of the servo to 90 degrees (Figure **48**).

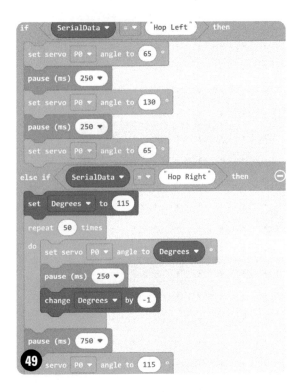

```
if    SerialData ▼  = ▼  " Hop Left "     then
    set servo  P0 ▼  angle to  65  °
    pause (ms)  250 ▼
    set servo  P0 ▼  angle to  130  °
    pause (ms)  250 ▼
    set servo  P0 ▼  angle to  65  °
else if    SerialData ▼  = ▼  " Hop Right "    then  ⊖
    set  Degrees ▼  to  115
    repeat  50  times
    do
        set servo  P0 ▼  angle to  Degrees ▼  °
        pause (ms)  250 ▼
        change  Degrees ▼  by  -1
    pause (ms)  750 ▼
    servo  P0 ▼  angle to  115  °
```

49

You can also set your code to do multiple moves when it recognizes a pose. Pretend you're the choreographer of a hit show and you're leading your robot dancers in their next set of dance moves (Figure **49**)!

You can also add some NeoPixels and have your dancer light up different colors for each move (Figure **50**).

```
serial on data received  new line ( ) ▼
    set  SerialData ▼  to  serial read until  new line ( ) ▼
    strip ▼  show color  red  pick random  1  to  255  green  pick random  1  to  255  blue  pick random  1  to  255
    if    SerialData ▼  = ▼  " Hop Left "    then
        set servo  P0 ▼  angle to  65  °
    else if    SerialData ▼  = ▼  " Hop Right "    then  ⊖
        set servo  P0 ▼  angle to  115  °
    if    SerialData ▼  = ▼  " Standing Still "    then  ⊖
```

50

Wow! Not only is this the final project in this chapter, it's also the final project of our maker journey together.

It's fitting that we ended this with a dance party. We've gotten you started on some amazing AI-powered robots in this chapter in hopes you'll be inspired to modify and create your own wondrous machines. So keep on tinkering, coding, and imagining, because the world is waiting for your fantastic ideas. Get ready to build a future full of wonder — the robot revolution starts with you!

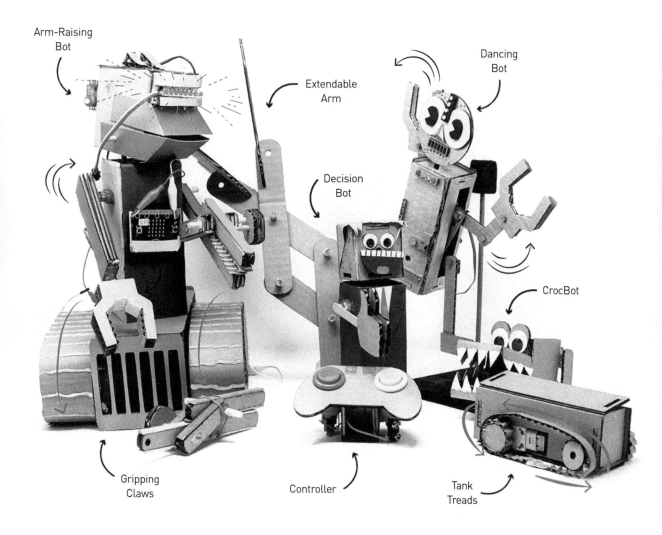

Arm-Raising Bot

Extendable Arm

Dancing Bot

Decision Bot

CrocBot

Gripping Claws

Controller

Tank Treads

READE RICHARD

is a maker educator and curriculum developer at Steamlabs, where he creates a wide range of micro:bit and AI-focused activities for classrooms across Canada. He has extensive experience teaching children and adults about technology, and serves on the board of directors for the Institute for Resource-Based Economy. Previously, Reade has helped develop maker spaces and activities for organizations such as the Ontario Science Centre, Association of Science and Technology Centres, and Western University. He lives in Toronto, Ontario.

BRENDA SHIVANANDAN

is a lead UX/UI designer at Steamlabs. With a focus on exhibit design and AI education, she has developed AI exhibits and workshops for Amazon Future Engineer and the Pacific Museum of Earth. Brenda has created illustrations and graphics for the Ontario Science Centre, Canadian Association of Science Centres, and the Toronto Metropolitan University. She lives in Mississaugas of the Credit, the Haudenosaunee, the Anishinaabe and the Huron-Wendat, in Treaty 13 (Toronto Purchase) territory.

ANDY FOREST

is the executive director of Steamlabs, and has built AI education experiences for Canada Learning Code, Amazon, the Ontario Science Centre, the Oslo Teknisk Museum, and many other organizations around the world. He has given talks and keynotes on the future of tech education to such organizations as the Canadian Internet Registration Authority, UNESCO, and the Ontario Ministry of Education. As a tech entrepreneur, Andy has led teams developing large AI machine-learning projects such as Berlitz's global online virtual classroom, which has served more than 2.5 million live student lessons over a 15-year period. He lives in Ottawa, Canada.

DENZEL EDWARDS

is a software developer, artist, and innovator, who uses his love of programming and complex problems to create applications that enable others to feel the same love for the future of technology as he does, while also teaching the value of ethical programming.

Milton Keynes UK
Ingram Content Group UK Ltd.
UKHW050939181123
432776UK00002B/3

9 781680 457292